✳✳ *JANE POWELL* ✳✳

THE WELL-LOVED STAR OF
SEVEN BRIDES FOR SEVEN BROTHERS
AND *ROYAL WEDDING* . . .
WHO WAS HERSELF A BRIDE
FOUR TIMES IN REAL LIFE. . . .

"Elizabeth (Taylor) . . . and I became friends . . .
Later she was a bridesmaid at my first wedding and then
I was a bridesmaid at *hers*. I'm certainly glad we stopped
that bridesmaid stuff—it could have become a full-time
career."

HOLLYWOOD'S WARMHEARTED DARLING WHO
DANCED BESIDE FRED ASTAIRE . . . YET NEVER
BELIEVED SHE WAS GOOD ENOUGH. . . .

"On November 5, 1949, I married Geary, my first husband.
It was a new adventure for both of us. I thought I loved him.
Maybe I did. But maybe I just wanted freedom, and a home
of my own, and babies."

STARDOM MADE HER, BUT SHE WOULDN'T LET
IT BEAT HER.

An honest and moving memoir of MGM's golden
era . . . through the eyes of one of its best-loved stars.

THE JANE POWELL STORY

THE GIRL NEXT DOOR... AND HOW SHE GREW

JANE POWELL

BERKLEY BOOKS, NEW YORK

This Berkley book contains the complete text
of the original hardcover edition. It has been
completely reset in a typeface designed
for easy reading, and was printed from new film.

THE JANE POWELL STORY:
THE GIRL NEXT DOOR . . . AND HOW SHE GREW

A Berkley Book / published by arrangement with
William Morrow & Company, Inc.

PRINTING HISTORY
William Morrow & Company edition 1988
Berkley edition / March 1990

ISBN: 0-425-11836-3

A BERKLEY BOOK® TM 757,375
Berkley Books are published by The Berkley Publishing Group,
200 Madison Avenue, New York, New York 10016.
The name "BERKLEY" and the "B" logo
are trademarks belonging to Berkley Publishing Corporation.

PRINTED IN THE UNITED STATES OF AMERICA

10 9 8 7 6 5 4 3 2 1

To Dick,
my companion of choice

✳ *ACKNOWLEDGMENTS* ✳

I FIND IT HARD to write acknowledgments. My life has been touched by so many people that if I mentioned them all, this book would be too long to read and too heavy to hold.

All of the people in my story, I acknowledge as a most important part of my life; and however they appear in these pages, I appreciate their presence, for without them, the "How She Grew" of me couldn't have been possible.

But there are some who inspired me to "put it all down" who do not appear. So to them a special hello: Pat Carroll, my friend who started me on this journey into the past; Harvey Klinger, my encouraging agent; Lisa Drew, my caring and talented editor, who kept things on the track.

I also wish to acknowledge Carol Sternhell, Helaine Feldman, and Lois Diane Hicks.

Life is a ladder that we all ascend
in a different way. Sometimes we run
up too fast and miss a few rungs.

** 1 **

THE LADY BEHIND me at the checkout counter of the supermarket in Wilton, Connecticut, introduced herself and said, "Last night I saw *Seven Brides for Seven Brothers* on television. It was such a pleasure seeing it again. Do you enjoy watching your old films?"

"Oh, no!" I told her. "You must watch *The Late Late Show*. I don't stay up that late."

What I didn't say is that I don't watch my old films on TV because I've always been too nervous and *embarrassed* to. Even today, in my late fifties, it bothers me to watch myself.

People are so nice. Not long ago I was hurrying—rushing, really—to a singing lesson in New York, when a man waiting in line at a movie theater caught my eye, and his face lit up as if he had seen a friend. He left his place in line and walked with me for several blocks, all the while talking and telling me how happy my films made him, how much joy—joy!—I had given him, recalling countless memories. I think of that conversation often. It's such a thrill to think I could have mattered to someone in that way, to a stranger, and yet not such a stranger at all.

The thing that amazes me about all this is that I haven't made a feature film in thirty years. I manage to keep busy, but I certainly don't think of myself as a movie star.

In fact, I never did, even when I was on the cover of *Life* magazine, or appearing in all those musicals for MGM. I guess I was too busy trying not to disappoint anybody ever to feel like one. The truth is that I never felt as if I really belonged in Hollywood, the Hollywood that took Suzanne Burce from Portland, Oregon, and turned her into Jane Powell. I *liked* Hollywood well enough, but I didn't feel any *connection* with it.

I've always been more interested in feelings than in things, and despite the fact that movies are about feelings, when it came to my personal life, I didn't know what to do with mine.

That's what this book is about—feelings. It seems to me there should be a reason for writing a book: self-help, literary value, advice. (I promise, *no advice*—after my four failed marriages, who'd want advice from me?) Of course, a book could be a novel. Certainly you could say my life as The Girl Next Door, Miss Goody Two-Shoes, was novel, or at least a novelty.

Most of the people who know me have always seen me as happy, bubbly, pert—all the adjectives bestowed upon me by the publicity department. Although I *do* have an optimistic outlook, I remember always crying as a child. Every picture taken of me shows me in tears and with a runny nose. My friend Roddy McDowall used to say that I cried at card tricks. I never thought of being sad. I never knew I was.

I *do* know I never wanted to be a movie star, but Mama and Daddy wanted me to be another Shirley Temple—parents did in those days—so dancing lessons and curly hair were on the agenda.

April Fool's Day, 1929, was my birthday, just six months before the start of the Great Depression.

As a child, I rarely had a party, probably because we didn't have the money and it was work for Mama. But there were a few lunches with tuna fish and noodles, and daffodils on the table. Daffodils are still my favorite flowers. They're so happy, and the first breath of spring.

One time, after I went to Hollywood, I got a collie pup, one of Lassie's, from the crew on my second picture, *Delightfully*

Dangerous. Oh, how I cried—with joy! How I had wanted a dog! We had always had cats because that's what Mama liked.

I don't remember having birthday cakes. Mama didn't like to cook, and she said her cakes always fell. But she did bake good pies.

On Sundays we had fried chicken, mashed potatoes, gravy, and peas eaten at four o'clock, at a card table in front of the radio as we listened to Jack Benny. That was the most special dinner we had. Even though Mama didn't like to cook, she did it until I took over, which I did at a very early age. I still love to cook. A friend recently described Thanksgiving at our house as a "cholesterol blowout."

When I was ten, I remember Daddy's boss came to dinner, and *I* cooked the meal. Mama helped me plan the menu. Somewhere I had read of mixing canned fruit cocktail and sherry together and serving it as an appetizer. I found some stem glasses and put the fruit and sherry in them, but because I didn't have plates under the glasses, there was no place to put the spoons when we were finished, so the tablecloth got dirty. I was so embarrassed. I had wanted everything to be perfect for Daddy's boss, who had come all the way from Pasadena, California. But nobody else seemed to know the difference.

I've always liked glasses with stems. They don't have to be expensive glasses, just as long as they have stems. Everything seems to taste better in them. Even today, many times I'm reminded of that embarrassed little girl with her cheap sherry and canned fruit cocktail in those stemmed glasses.

I was so young when I started my Shirley Temple lessons, I couldn't have known what was going on. I started dancing at the age of two, soon after I learned to walk. Mama said, "You used to tap out the beat on the hearth; you were so smart for your age." Some of my earliest memories are of the dance costumes Mama made for me—"dress up" to a little girl. Once I was a pussycat in light brown velvet and peach satin paws and ears. The pussycat hat made my face itch and I couldn't hear, but I still remember my song, "Sitting on the Backyard Fence": "Meow, meow, the pussycats are calling, waiting for you to come out. Come out, come out, the pussycats are calling, sitting on the backyard fence." I felt like a real cat in itchy peach-colored ears and a long, fuzzy tail. Maybe I was four. The recital was in a school, and I can still smell the brown linoleum that had been cleaned with the usual wintergreen-smelling solution they used in schools, and see the rows of desks in the schoolroom where we changed, attended by eager stage mothers. Everyone was so excited! Some little children cried or wet their pants. I probably did both.

I danced and sang like Shirley Temple, they said. I even had Shirley Temple curls, like all the other little moppets. But my hair was really straight and brown. God made a mistake there, so I had my first permanent when I was two years old, and many more after that. I cried through the whole operation. It took place at a salon at somebody's house. I had to sit on telephone books because I was so small, and my feet stuck straight out in front of me, as stiff as a board. In those days they put a big, heavy contraption over your head, with lots of wires and clamps hanging down. It looked like some weird animal. I was frightened. It burned my ears and made funny hissing, gurgling noises. No wonder I cried. When the perm had grown out, Mama would sit me on the drainboard and curl my hair with the curling iron, rolling my straight brown hair over her finger and burning my ear at the same time, and I'd cry again.

I cried a lot as a baby. Every time I looked at that camera, I howled. I think I must have come from the womb that way. There was a reason I cried so much. There was something wrong, I felt, something very deep inside. But that's a hard subject to face, and it took me most of my life to face it.

I don't know why other people saw me as the Shirley Temple type. I had no blond curly hair or even a hint of a dimple, but I did dance and sing. I never looked good with dark hair, but I didn't realize that until MGM started bleaching it for my first Technicolor picture. I should have been born a blonde, then maybe my name would have been Shirley.

I felt lonely as a child. I don't remember Mama ever playing with me, but we were always together. I don't know what we did all day. I do know I always wore white shoes, and it seems to me she was either polishing my shoes, or curling my hair, or both. I was her doll, her toy. We moved a great deal when I was young, so it was hard to make friends. In every new neighborhood everyone was always older or younger. I went to three different grade schools in three years, and attended one of them twice. We always seemed to live farther away from the school than any of the other kids, always on the boundary of this school district or that one. I would walk with my class-mates on my way home, but no one ever came the distance with me. They went to each other's houses but rarely visited mine—too far, always too far away.

No matter where we moved I always took myself to Sunday school. I didn't care what church it was. I just loved to color in the picture books about Jesus—Jesus riding a donkey, Jesus talking to the children. That's my strongest memory of Sunday school, those bright crayons and donkeys. I also liked being with the other children there, surrogate brothers and sisters. I never went to nursery school because Mama didn't want me to. She said, "It will take you away from me." I wonder. . . . Even today, I don't know how to play games, maybe because I never played them as a child. In fact, I used to say to my father when he went to work, "Daddy, please buy me a brother or sister"—at Fred Meyer, the biggest grocery store in Port-land. And every night, he'd come home and say, "Oh, Squirrely, I forgot again," and I'd be so disappointed. I wanted one so badly.

I was very isolated, I realize now. I never saw how other families worked, how they related—only what I saw in the movies. I didn't know what was normal. I rarely slept overnight at anyone's house because I wet the bed. Of course, lots of children do that, but no one told me—I thought I was the only one in the world.

There weren't many relatives around, either. They mainly lived in Tacoma, and we lived in Portland. We would spend Christmas with Mama's family, the Bakers. I had three cousins I was close to, but there was something about their families that I didn't understand at the time. They were never happy for anyone else's success or accomplishment. They never said anything nice about each other, and I was following suit. If someone got a new car they'd say, "Oh, it's a nice car, I suppose, but why should they have something that big. It's disgusting." When I went to Hollywood, even with my three cousins I was so fond of it was, "Oh, we'll never hear from *her* again." They were very supportive as long as you were down on your luck, but as soon as you started climbing up, they'd say, "Humph, it's nice but . . ." just like Mama.

The tone was always negative; everything that was said was negative, even the good-byes. They used to call them the "Baker Good-byes." Nobody ever wanted to leave because they knew if they left they'd be talked about. And it was true. In fact, we laughed about it. "Well, good-bye, honey," someone would say. "Well, good-bye, honey," another would say; and then there'd be kisses, *wet kisses*, galore. Those who were left would sit down and talk about whoever had gone.

But Uncle Herb was different; he was my drinking uncle. I loved him; he was so funny. Many times he would drop Christmas presents in the mud on his way to the Christmas gathering—if he'd remember them at all. Once my uncle Lynn said, "Herb, someday you're going to end up in the gutter." Herb's reply was "Well, at least I'll have running water."

It seems to me that Mama and I stayed home a lot in a small apartment with a green kitchen. For some reason our kitchens seemed to be painted pea green, with the table and chairs in the same color, and furnished by Sears, Roebuck. Mama wasn't one to go to museums or explore, or do much of anything. She wasn't interested.

When I was of school age, my happiest time was September, when I could go back to school; not that I was a good student, but it gave me someplace to go. Most kids loved summer vacations, but I hated them. I can't remember ever doing anything in the summer; except once I went to camp for five days and cried twenty hours a day, stopping only to eat. I didn't know anyone at the camp, and, of course, crying all the time didn't make me the most desirable, fun-loving girl to be around; so I went home.

When I was five I started appearing on a kiddie radio program called *Stars of Tomorrow*, an amateur show. No doubt

I auditioned for it, but I don't remember; however, I can still picture the man who hosted it, Nate Cohen. He was round-faced and dark-haired with glasses and very, *very* jolly. Uncle Nate. I sang and danced. You couldn't see me, but you sure could hear me. After a while, I had a regular slot on that show. (Daddy let everyone in town know I was on the radio!) I would sing the Hit Parade songs, like "On the Good Ship Lollipop." But my favorite was "Playmate, come out and play with me, And bring your dollies three, Climb up my apple tree, Slide down my rain barrel, Knock on my cellar door, And we'll be jolly friends, forevermore."

Jolly friends, forevermore. I guess that was the part I liked.

I don't remember learning anything about singing until much, much later. I just sang like most children. I took every kind of dancing lesson at Agnes Peters Dancing School, *the* dancing school in Portland—acrobatic, tap, ballet—but I don't know if I learned any technique, I just did it by rote. I was very quick to learn and could pick up a song or dance step the first time I heard or saw it.

Why was I dancing in school auditoriums and singing on the radio? I don't know. Perhaps it was something I did for my parents. And it *was* fun. I guess I never had fantasies about becoming a star; I just wanted to please. In fact, part of why I got along so well with my parents was that I always did what I was told. I didn't ask why—I never questioned *anything*. That lasted for too many years. I just did it, because it was there, and I was supposed to. It's only recently that I've come to realize how terribly important all this was to my parents, much more so than I ever realized.

A while ago my mother and I were having an argument—a discussion?—and she said, "Well, *I* never wanted you to be in show business. It was your father." And I asked her, "Why did you give me the lessons? Why did we leave Portland? Why didn't we stay there?" She couldn't answer.

We first left Portland when I was six. There I was, taking dancing lessons from Agnes Peters, performing in recitals, and all of a sudden a man appeared at the dancing school. He was Scotty Weston, a promoter obviously, a talent scout and dance teacher, he said, from Oakland, California. He was in Portland looking for promising children—to make one a "star." He chose me. The plan was we would go to Oakland and he would give me lessons—not for free, mind you—and then he would get me into the movies. My parents thought Oakland was Hollywood. After all, it was in California, and California was the promised land, so Weston was a dream come true.

We went to Oakland. Just like that. The worst part was, Daddy even quit his job. He'd been with the Wonder Bread Company for fourteen years and he left them so we could move to Oakland, so I could, would, become another Shirley Temple. The company even gave him the gold watch. Daddy was a bit worried. He said to Herb, "What if we have to come back?" And Uncle Herb quipped, "Well, just walk in backward and they'll never know you left."

We went south to Oakland in May, Mama, my grandmother Cary, and me. Daddy came later. We lived in one room in a tiny hotel with a rollaway bed, and I slept on the couch. We cooked on a hot plate—we had to sneak it in. NO COOKING IN THE ROOMS the sign read. Our best meal was toast and hot chocolate. I was a chocoholic for years. I would put chocolate on corn flakes, if there were any. I can still smell the toast burning and feel the butter crawling down my arm as I ate before my classes. I was a very nervous child and scrawny. I hardly ate anything for fear of throwing up. I can remember we would eat one meal in a little tearoom near the dance class sometimes, tuna fish sandwiches and vegetable soup, but I could never eat for fear of getting sick. I'd take one bite, get up from the table, and walk around the block. I ate all my meals like that for years.

Tuna and soup, cocoa and toast—that's all I remember eating. I had such a terrible fear of throwing up. It seemed like the worst thing that could happen to me. I wouldn't even go to parties because I knew I would have to have food. As a matter of fact, I carried this fear with me even when I started dating: I would take along a bottle of Pepto-Bismol with me no matter where we went. I'd order dinner, the cheapest on the menu so I would not be embarrassed when I didn't eat. Then I'd take one bite of something, drink some tea and possibly a swig of Pepto. It wasn't to stay thin. I was just afraid of becoming sick and being mortified.

So there I was in Oakland, eating toast and walking around the block. In the daytime I had dance classes with Scotty Weston in an enormous, dimly lighted rented ballroom filled with kids tapping and mothers tapping right along with them while they knitted, talked, or both. The mothers sat like crows on a fence, watching and waiting, ready to pounce on anyone who got in their little one's way. It was a gruesome sight. The ballroom where we danced was dark and cavernous—it was dark probably to save electricity—and heavy green curtains hung everywhere. This fiasco lasted three months. Suddenly, it was all over; I hadn't been discovered, of course. Weston disappeared, our money ran out, and I had a "dry spell," washed up at six.

We went back to Portland, but we didn't walk in backward as Uncle Herb had suggested. Now Daddy couldn't get a job. There was none to be had. We rented another one-bedroom apartment (this time my parents slept on the daybed in the living room), and I started school. But pretty soon we had to move; we couldn't pay the rent.

Luckily for us, some friends who managed an apartment building, the Banbury Cross, let us have an apartment there. Daddy tried to sell pots and pans, Tupperware, anything—he was a very industrious man, anything but lazy—but he didn't have much luck. He even tried shoveling snow, but there isn't any in Portland. Finally when our friends left, Mama and Daddy got the manager's apartment and the job. The Banbury Cross was where people encouraged my career. There were thirty-six apartments, two apartments on the ground floor. There was a buzzer on the front door, that echoed throughout the vestibule. There was brown linoleum in the small foyer, and a sectioned glass door with see-through dusty curtains attached from top to bottom, separating the dull outside from the dark inside. There was a pay telephone attached to the outside wall of our apartment where tenants could call out and receive calls. We would answer their calls and buzz them to come to the phone. The phone was always busy and we were always pushing buttons to let someone in, or someone was always calling Daddy to come running to fix something.

This red-brick, nondescript apartment house, whose name was more interesting than the building itself, was our home for more years than I care to recall. The bleakness of the outside could never surpass the dark depression of the inside. It looked as if I had drawn its childlike architecture. Four stories, square windows, two to each apartment on the front, square in every way. Not a round corner could be found except for the broken bricks that had been bruised by a runaway bicycle or a baby carriage. A strip of green lawn at the curb and a cement driveway bordered one side, the side we lived on separating it from the apartment next door. Cement was everywhere. When the sun did shine, it all seemed white and sterile. That was the Banbury Cross. I often wondered why they picked the romantic fairy-tale name of "Banbury Cross" for such an uninteresting stack of bricks. Last time I was in Portland I saw it quite by chance, and it looks the same, only smaller—but just as depressing.

We got our rent free and thirty-five dollars a month. My job was to help Daddy empty the garbage cans. We would collect the small cans from each tenant's door, empty them, line them with newspapers, and then I'd return them to the tenants. All the time I'd be singing. Apparently the tenants were listening and kept insisting to my parents, "You've got to give that girl singing lessons." Now I don't know if this was to shut me up or to encourage a career, but eventually my parents scrimped and saved, and at ten I started Shirley Temple-ing again.

Oakland had really stunned my parents, I think, and left them reeling. Something so hopeful, a promise of transformation for them had turned so quickly into emotional and financial disaster. Their most brilliant career move, the plan to assure their daughter's future, *their* future, suddenly looked stupid. We really struggled for the next few years, but they never gave up. People have asked, "How did you get into show business?" Well, I fulfilled my parents' dreams.

My Saturday-morning singing lessons were way downtown,

and I took the Broadway streetcar by myself to sing for Mrs. Fred L. Olson, my first teacher. I felt so efficient and proud, going off with my brown leatherette case with the disappearing handles and my initials S. L. B. for Suzanne Lorraine Burce, on the front. Mrs. Olson was a pretty grandmother type, and I liked her, but when I couldn't sing something right, I'd get a knot in my stomach (I still do) and sometimes break into tears.

I learned most of the typical soprano songs: "Il Baccio," "Indian Love Call," "Donkey Serenade." I also learned that opera was not to my taste, but I loved the arias, particularly Puccini's because he was so romantic. The first opera I saw was *Madame Butterfly*, and I cried, but I could cry even when I was happy.

Our apartment building really got its fill of me and "Il Baccio," I'm sure. Daddy bought or rented a spinet so I could practice, and I sang all the time, but I never did learn to play or read music. Music is mathematical, and math is something I've never been able to master. Fortunately, I have a quick ear, but so much of what a singer should know I never learned.

What else do I remember? What else do I know of the streetcars and the garbage cans and the music? What else can I tell you about Suzanne?

Well, as a child I loved anything pretty, especially clothes or jewelry. I was a gypsy, Mama used to say, with rings, bracelets, anything that glittered—and I liked a lot of them. Mama made most of my clothes when I was little, until she got too nervous to sew anymore. And she sewed beautifully. I remember one dress she made. It was two pieces; I had designed it in taffeta with small red and white checks. The skirt was full, the overblouse had a square neck and big puffed sleeves, and it had a bustle and ruffles up the back—and I glued sequins into every square of that dress! That was a very popular style at the time, and it looks like it's coming back again. But I have no intention of gluing little sequins onto anything ever again!

I loved clothes (I still do) and I loved to design them (I still do) but as a young girl I never felt I had enough to wear. I can remember walking to school with my friend Patty Melvin: We

were in fourth or fifth grade and it was still warm, so it must
have been September. I can still see us, walking on the shady
side of the street, and I can still picture Patty's new beige skirt
and matching sweater. Patty was on the plump side, but I
envied her, her house, her sister, her pretty clothes. As we
walked she told me her mother had bought her a red and brown
skirt, too, with matching sweaters, and she had two pairs of
school shoes. I thought she must be the richest girl in the
world!

Like all little girls at that time, I had paper dolls, but I didn't
play with them—I designed new clothes for them. I never
played with dolls, but with paper, pencil, and crayon I'd be
contented for hours. I thought dolls were silly; it was silly to
talk to them: "It's time to go to the ball, Patsy Ann." Ugh.
Fantasy didn't appeal to me. I couldn't fantasize. What I liked
was washing and ironing their clothes and doing it again and
again. To me, that was doing something.

For a while I was just a girl cutting out paper-doll clothes
and taking singing lessons, but not for long. By the time I was
eleven I was performing again.

A local promoter, Carl Werner, had taken over my career;
and because of him, when I was twelve I was selected as the
Oregon Victory Girl. This happened during the war—the
Second World War, not the First. My job was to travel around
the state singing and selling victory bonds, anything for the
cause. I'm not certain how I actually got the job, but I'm pretty
sure no money was involved. At least not for me. I did it for
almost two years. In the winter, when I was in school, I would
do the Kiwanis Clubs and the Rotary Clubs, many groups like
that. In the summer I would go to different towns and sing at
war bond rallies, army camps, and naval installations, at
veterans' homes and hospitals. This would usually take all
summer, and I enjoyed it; it gave me something to do. I
enjoyed the traveling, enjoyed meeting people. I even chris-
tened a warship once, the *Peter Skene Ogden*. It sank!

One time, Lana Turner came to town and I presented her
with a bouquet of roses and sang my victory songs. I was
terribly excited to meet her—and I can even remember what

she wore, a suite with a black and white polka-dot blouse, a hat, and a fur. She was a "sweater girl" all right. Her image was there—right in front. I went home afterward and lay in bed wondering what she was doing at that exact moment, trying to picture her life, her glamorous life. A couple of years later I met her again at MGM, but she didn't remember me, of course. In fact, I met her many times after that and she *never* remembered who I was. Every time I'd say, "Oh, yes, we've met before, many times."

During those same years, I had two weekly radio shows of my own. On the first one I sang with an organ accompaniment once a week on KOIN Radio. It was sponsored by Zell Brothers jewelry store. Eight dollars a week, fifteen minutes of song. I loved my theme song, an old song, "For You." ("There's nothing in this world I wouldn't do, For you, For you."). Later I did an hour show with an orchestra and other performers on Sunday nights. It was unusual for someone so young to have a show, but it all seemed very normal to me and fun.

Radio was spectacular in those days, like television today. The big shows I did later, like *The Railroad Hour, Lux Radio Theater,* and *The Chase and Sanborn Hour with Edgar Bergen and Charlie McCarthy,* all had their own orchestras. All the big stations—and the one in Portland was comparatively big—had their own staffs, orchestras, and companies of stars. Radio had a mystery about it. I would listen to *I Love a Mystery* and the children's shows on Saturday mornings and try to visualize what the prince or princess looked like. Very rarely did you see pictures of radio personalities in magazines or papers. It was all a fantasy: You could fantasize whatever you liked. It was exciting. It still is to me.

We stayed at the Banbury Cross for four or five years—with me no doubt driving the tenants crazy with all that warbling— but by the time I was thirteen and still the Oregon Victory Girl, my parents had bought a house. Daddy was selling baby food then, for Clapp's Baby Foods, and he was doing quite well. I actually had my own bedroom, and Mama made a skirt for the kidney-shaped dressing table Daddy had bought at an unfinished furniture store. It was white organdy with eyelet ruffles. I felt like a princess, and oh so posh. Finally we had a house.

How I wanted to be normal or ordinary, and enter Grant High School. But I was always being pulled out of school to perform somewhere. I was always set apart from the other kids, and I worked *so hard* not to be stuck-up.

I did have one girlfriend in the seventh and eighth grades, Nancy Lee Dixon; later her married name was Huntzinger. I was very close to her. She was very sweet. We kept in contact until a few years ago when she passed away. Of course, she lived on one side of the school and I lived on the other; but at least we went to the movies together on Saturday afternoons. I even started spending Saturday nights over at her house after my bedwetting stopped. I don't believe she ever stayed at our house, though. Mama didn't really like having children around.

I was sort of popular with some of the other girls, but I always felt they were looking down their noses at me: "Oh, she has to go do *that* again, she has to go *perform*." But worst of all was performing at school. Oh, how I *hated* that. Standing in front of my peers was very difficult. Even today it's difficult for me because I want to be so good. Kids are very cruel to each other; they're jealous, sarcastic, rude. I would do anything to get out of performing in school. Anything.

I just wanted to be one of the gang, but I never knew where the gang went because I was always away working. Usually the job would be to sing at a luncheon meeting, from twelve to two, so by the time I got back there would be a half hour of school left. That sort of thing didn't go over too well with the other kids. I didn't think I was special, just different. But I didn't like that difference.

It was an odd life really. I was different but eager to be ordinary. Now here I am, years later, looking through a scrapbook that was started forty-six years ago, seeing a program from a voice recital when I was ten in which I sang "Il Baccio": I'm also looking at the thanks I got from many Rotary Clubs; newspaper clippings about my war-bond effort (the navy made me an honorary recruiting officer); a picture of me with Lana Turner; a thank-you note from the president of Northwestern Electric Company (for singing on their radio program); a photograph of me in my winter Victory Girl outfit (a red, white, and blue uniform); a get-well letter from the mayor of Portland (when I came down with the measles); things I had almost forgotten. And I'm wondering: Was that me?

** 2 **

When Paul E. Burce married petite Eileen Baker in Portland on May 12, 1928 (not a good year for marrying, it seems), I doubt they were thinking about tiny movie stars as they walked down that aisle, an eager and innocent young couple. I'm not sure Mama even wanted children.

I am sure they were thinking about romance, love forever, and a future together. They must have been so glad they had met, so glad he had moved to Portland from Shaunavon, Saskatchewan, Canada, and she from Tacoma, Washington. Neither of them could have anticipated the years of struggling to pay the rent, Daddy's job delivering Wonder Bread, Mama's tiredness or boredom (evidently she was always taking naps), their increasingly frequent arguments and eventual divorce. Neither of them could have imagined that someday they'd have a daughter who would dance with Fred Astaire.

Even when I was very small, my parents didn't get along. It isn't so much the fighting I remember, though there was that, it was the terrible "silent times" when Mama wouldn't speak to Daddy for days. Daddy wasn't a fighter, I guess, and that made Mama angry, so she'd give him the silent treatment, and I was translator. Sometimes the best way to win is not to say anything, to freeze the other person out with your anger—and she knew how to do that. I hated being shut out.

It seemed to me as if Daddy could never do anything right as far as she was concerned. "He isn't working hard enough," Mama would say. "He's working *too* hard." "He's always in the yard." "He doesn't know how to have fun."

Even when things were going right, something was wrong. With Mama there was always a "but." It was a lovely day, but . . . He works hard, but . . . She's pretty, but . . . And on and on and on. It was like the famous "Baker Good-bye." There was always a complaint somewhere in the air, always a little dig, a twist of the knife, a hurt.

Complaints or not, when I was a child, I adored Mama. She was my best friend, my closest companion, my chum. I loved Daddy, too—but it was Mama who spent time with me, Mama I depended on. We were the Bobbsey Twins, allies, two little girls holding hands. She was a little girl herself, only four feet eleven.

I never heard Mama say anything really nice about anyone. The awful thing was I'd find myself doing the same thing, giving people the silent treatment, being critical, just like Mama. For years I found something wrong with everybody. Thank heavens that is in the past.

Sometimes I see other traits in myself that remind me of Mama. I guess that's to be expected, but as I've told my children, if you're going to emulate someone, always make it the best part of that person, not the worst.

Mama was one of seven children, the baby, so she was always cuddled and fussed over, spoiled really. When I was little I used to wonder why everyone, including me, always tried so hard to please her, why everyone went around on tiptoe trying to pacify my mama. She was used to it. Mama was a very pretty, strong-willed woman, and she scared Daddy and me. She would suddenly, unpredictably, get upset and silent and wouldn't talk for days.

My grandmother Cary, Mama's mama, was another strong lady. I don't think she wanted to be a grandma either, because everyone called her "Ma Baker." She didn't tote a gun, but she was tough and smart. She went to college, which was unheard of in those days, and started smoking at seventy-three, not that

that was so smart, but she had a mind of her own. For some reason she never wanted me to know that she smoked. But the cigarette burns in her clothes were a dead giveaway. According to one of our family stories, Ma's father was a judge in La Grande, Oregon, and wrote some of Susan B. Anthony's speeches. I don't know if this really happened, but it gives you an idea of what sort of upbringing Ma had. It's no wonder she went to college! She married her first cousin, or her third cousin, depending on whom you believe.

Ma and my mother were very close, Mama being her baby, and she adored me, her baby's baby. I remember her always holding court, always talking—she had such strong opinions about absolutely everything! She was a staunch Republican, and unless you were a Republican, too, she wouldn't talk to you. Ma was very pretty, just like Mama, and I loved her.

It was odd, but Mama, Daddy, my grandmother, and I all looked alike. Mama and Daddy could have been brother and sister. They were both little, with round faces, small hands and feet. In fact, although we all looked alike, they were rounder all over. Daddy was plump with crinkly blue eyes, thinning hair with canals running back, even when he was young. His hair kept thinning but it never disappeared, it just turned gray.

Mama was often shy with strangers, but not with Daddy and me. Ever since I was born she'd struggled with her weight—she always blamed me for this problem. She used to weigh about 128 pounds, and sometimes said, "When I was pregnant I looked just like an old-fashioned milk bottle, with a round top and bottom, like a sausage tied in the middle, and I can't lose it." And ever since then, she counted calories. I do not come from thin or tall or willowy stock.

When I gain weight, I get depressed. I try to keep my weight between ninety-four and ninety-six pounds, and I usually do, but I watch it a bit. It used to be a fetish with me. I'd wake up in the morning, look at my stomach and arms (which had a tendency to fatten up), and plan my eating for the day. After every meal I'd put my hands on my waist and feel how fat I was and proceed to get depressed. That was *every day.*

Sometimes I wouldn't go to a party because I felt fat . . .

possibly I was two pounds overweight. I thought everyone would think, "What a *slob* she is." I counted calories even before I was a teenager, following in Mama's footsteps. Dieting is such a bore that I don't let it get out of hand. I exercise almost every day and I try not to waste calories; there's nothing worse to me than wasting calories eating food that doesn't taste good. If it isn't delicious, I don't bother. My credo is: There'll always be another chocolate cake!

My grandfather, Mama's daddy, was the only tall one in the family. He was six feet and more, but no one got any of those genes. Grandpa died when I was exactly two—in fact, Mama said she had just bought me a birthday cake—so I don't remember him at all. Mama says he was a bartender on a ship; my cousin Barbara says he was head of the ship's store, which sounds more elite. It's funny how people like Grandpa, our inheritance really, just fade away. I do know he sailed out of Seattle; they would shanghai men from the docks and shove off for China. Obviously he did come home once in a while to sire seven children. All his.

Daddy's mother, my grandmother Nellie, I remember very well. She lived in Seattle, so I didn't see her that often, but I remember she used to bake cookies—something Mama never did—and let me cut them out. Those times with Grandma Nellie seemed very special, unusual, and exciting. Maybe my interest in cooking comes from those wonderful afternoons with Grandma Nellie. To this day, I know I loved rolling out cookie dough and turning it into animals and stars.

Grandma Nellie was a devout Methodist. She wouldn't tolerate alcohol; she wouldn't even have a bottle of vanilla in the house, Mama said. She was a stern, serious woman—she didn't believe in dancing or playing cards. She wore round-rimmed glasses, which made her look like a picture you might see in the front hall of an orphanage, very stoic, very severe, plainly dressed. Daddy's father, my grandpa John, divorced her after thirty-five years—no wonder—and that was unusual in those days. Grandpa just got tired of all that seriousness, I guess. He was a carpenter and loved to sing; that's how I remember him, laughing and singing. He remarried, a sweet woman named Julia who loved his singing—and his laughing, too.

Daddy's brother, Uncle Ralph, was very different from him, unfriendly, selfish, and gay. Daddy always said Ralph was his mother's favorite. He never really worked, played the piano for himself only, and collected things—buttons and laces. I'm not sure how he supported himself. For a while he was a nudist, and ate crackers in bed. He and Daddy shared a bed when they were young, even after Daddy had started working at the age of eight. Whenever he'd come home, Daddy said, there would always be crumbs in the bed and Ralph would be asleep. However, that's all I know about Ralph: He was Grandma's favorite, played the piano, and ate crackers in bed.

Sometimes when I think about my childhood, which I've been doing a lot lately, I remember aunts, uncles, cousins, and grandmas, but my strongest feeling is one of loneliness. I remember Daddy's gentle warmth. Occasionally, on a Sunday morning, Daddy would take me by the hand and say, "Come on, Squirrely, let's me and you have a party," and off we would go to the beer parlor. He'd stand me on top of the table, and I'd sing his favorite song, with all the gestures: "A Shanty in Old Shanty Town." There was no one else there but us; it was our time together. Sometimes he'd let me have a nickel glass of beer and he'd have a dime glass. And then we'd go home. I can still smell that sweet beer.

Daddy always made everyone feel comfortable and important. When I was a baby, he threw me up in the air to make me giggle, and took my hand as we walked along. I loved him, but it also seems as if I hardly knew him then. He was always working, so I didn't have the camaraderie with him I had with Mama. And when I remember how loving Mama was, how she picked me up when I cried, hugged and kissed me, I don't understand why I was unhappy. It's hard to understand how things got so bad that Mama and I barely spoke for years. If Mama was loving once, why did I feel lonely and isolated?

We really had been so close, always together, inseparable really. She stayed with me while I was working or at my lessons and traveled with me when I went on the road.

I loved my father, but it wasn't a "Daddy's girl" kind of thing. We always got along. I loved him, but most of all I didn't want to take sides. Because Daddy was working, he'd be gone all day and I'd spend the time with Mama. Later, when I was making movies, it was Mama who stayed at the studio with me, not Daddy. It was a state law in California that a parent or guardian had to be present while a child actor was performing, but I didn't mind—I liked having Mama around.

I think the quality time parents speak of today is very important. I didn't know about "quality time" then. Daddy would come home, he'd be tired, we'd have dinner, and everyone would go to bed by ten o'clock. We never played games, rarely discussed things, or played cards, although Mama played a little bridge when I was young, but I never learned how to. My parents didn't read much, either. Mama would occasionally read a novel, but I don't come from a reading family. The only time I got to play games was at my grandma Nellie's where we'd only play Sorry, never Monopoly—just Sorry.

Quite honestly, I'm not sure what my parents taught me. They took me to Hollywood, certainly, and I'm glad of that, but I don't remember them actually teaching me anything. I don't remember any words of wisdom except for Mama's famous warning about dust: "Collect something and it collects dust." I was never given any words to live by or special messages to recall from Mama or Daddy—just dust! I missed that.

Everything I learned, I learned by watching—how to use the right knife and fork, whatever. Somehow I just sensed when something was wrong. I remember photographers came to the house once to take some of those terrible posed pictures of our family for one of the movie magazines. It was early in my career and they took one photograph that still embarrasses me. It was a picture of Daddy leaning his elbows on the table, shirtsleeves and hairy amrs, trying to *stab* the butter with his knife. His approach to butter seemed normal to me at the time, but when I saw the picture I knew somehow it was wrong.

Things were never explained to me. I had no idea when to

shave my legs or under my arms, or even if this was done. Mama didn't do it, I guess. I wasn't aware that shaving was something girls did, and I didn't find out until I was in a movie and the choreographer, Nick Castle, had to *tell* me. In a dance number in *Nancy Goes to Rio*, I had to raise my arms above my head. He suggested tactfully, "Don't you think you should shave?" It was the first time someone had ever mentioned it to me. I was terribly embarrassed that someone, and a man at that, had to tell me.

Certainly Mama had never told me about anything, including sex. I was very afraid of sex, and knew absolutely nothing about it. My girlfriend, Nancy Lee Dickson, once said to me when we were in the eighth grade, "Just ask your mother, Suzanne. She'll tell you all about it." By my mother was the last person I could ask anything like that.

One day I was sitting in our big overstuffed rocking chair reading the label on a Listerine bottle. I must have had a sore throat; I seemed to have sore throats quite often. As I was reading, I asked Mama what d-o-u-c-h-e meant. She turned pale, got up, and ran out of the room. It must be dirty and have something to do with sex, I thought, so I never asked her again. What terrible, sordid thoughts I imagined.

When I was twelve and first started menstruating, I had no idea what was happening to me. I was terrified—I thought I had sat on some glass. Mama ran around the house, wringing her hands and saying, "My poor baby, my poor baby," and I thought I must have done something bad and was going to die—but I didn't.

I would never have asked Daddy any of these questions, of course. Girls and their daddies didn't talk about things like that then.

Daddy was Santa Claus. I mean, he was so thoughtful and good and giving. Santa and Mr. Fix-It, he could fix *anything*, including broken hearts. The household phrase when I was small was "Daddy fix." I remember the time he fixed up a special Christmas present. I had wanted a bicycle desperately. I needed one to get to school, since we lived so far away, but money was tight and I didn't really expect to get it. But Daddy found an old bike, a real "fix-me-up," advertised for five dollars in a newspaper, and went to work. He straightened and painted over all the dents and scars, rubbed and polished.

But I was so disappointed. It was a boy's bike without balloon tires like all the other kids had and, worst of all, it wasn't red, it was black. Black! (probably to cover all the scratches). It was certainly a big surprise in every way. I never told Daddy how disappointed I was. I felt terrible to feel that way because I knew he had worked so hard. I rode that black bike to school every day, not even holding on to the handle-bars. Just like a boy.

Daddy loved Christmas. He got more excited than I did, which may be another reason I think of him as Santa. He could never wait until Christmas morning to open gifts. He would wake me up the night before, get me out of bed, and make me open my presents. Every year I begged him to let me wait until morning so I would have something to do on Christmas Day, but he never could wait. He really couldn't.

Easter was another story. I loved Easter. I never quite believed in Santa Claus because we didn't have a chimney, but the Easter bunny was very real to me. He could show up anywhere. He didn't need a special entrance.

One Easter—oh, do I ever remember this one!—I got up early and tiptoed into the living room. Mama and Daddy were still asleep on the Murphy bed. I don't know if the bunny had arrived or not, but I remember braiding every hair on Daddy's head while he slept and tying each braid with different colored ribbons. That was the only time I can remember getting a spanking from him. He was so mad—but he did look funny and cute with those little braids sticking out like colored porcupine needles.

I associated Daddy with happy things, like holidays and good smells. Because he worked for the Wonder Bread Company, he smelled so good when he came home.

Happy times and warm bread—yes, I *do* remember those. But I also remember the other days. I remember Mama drinking, for instance; it was only on Saturday nights, but those nights were disasters. I hardly understood what was happening, but it frightened me. She could never handle alcohol, and later it almost killed her. I also remember—but vaguely—that Mama and Daddy separated a few times. I don't know why, and I don't know why they got back together. It upset me, but I was so busy working I didn't stop to think much about it, or maybe the fog just shrouds the pain. I was always very good at not thinking too hard about anything, or things, particularly things I wasn't supposed to know about.

There was a lot I wasn't supposed to know, and a lot of questions I didn't ask. My childhood seems like a faraway picture now. I try to color in the blanks, but it's hard. I do recall the warm bread, the cold silence, and the boozy Saturday nights, a frightened child being suffocated with a pillow . . .

Suffocated with a pillow?! That didn't happen. It couldn't have happened! Mama, did it happen?

I'm not that frightened child anymore, but I sometimes feel angry, and guilty about my feelings about Mama.

She has a remarkable way of turning things around. If something starts out one way, it will end up differently by the time she's finished—and you don't know how in the world it happened. It's miraculous. She picks up words that have nothing to do with the subject you're talking about, so you completely forget what the subject was. She can start out saying, "Well, the dress was blue," and you say, "No, Mama, the dress was green." And by the time you're finished, you're saying blue and she's saying green! It's a fascinating process, like a train disappearing in a tunnel and coming out backward. It happens many times when she doesn't like the way a conversation is going.

When I got married for the first time, Mama divorced me. *Mama,* my closest companion. She had housed herself in me, then left, deserted, and divorced me. She said, "You won't have time for me anymore." She was my best friend—and suddenly she was gone. I felt like a twenty-one-year-old orphan. The desertion was very hard to understand, and because of it I learned not to hold on to anything too closely, even my children. Particularly my children. Soon afterward, she divorced Daddy, too. She said they'd only stayed together because of me. That put such a burden on me, I swore I'd never do that to *my* children. I still don't really understand what happened. Maybe she was jealous of my happiness, or maybe she was expecting rejection.

One time when Mama was in her fifties (she's over eighty now) I took her to dinner at Chasen's, an elegant Los Angeles restaurant, for her birthday. I'd recently been to Europe with my second husband, and had bought her a very pretty gold ring—at least I thought it was pretty. She immediately told me it was wrong and didn't fit. She started screaming at me, and I started crying. It seemed that I could never do anything right in her eyes.

For a long time Mama and I didn't see each other much. I was appearing in *The Unsinkable Molly Brown* at the Circle Theater in San Carlos, California, and she was living not too far away, so I invited her to come to opening night. She did, but she had been drinking. Ever since childhood, I had hated being around anyone who'd been drinking, especially Mama. Her wig was all askew and her eyes were almost crossed; two people were holding her up when she came to my dressing room, along with her third husband, George Snow. I asked Mama if she liked the show, and she answered, "I didn't understand it; it was too sophisticated for me. And why didn't you sing in it?" I said, "I thought I did." I raised my voice in anger and lost my temper. She left. I wrote her a letter later that said, "Mama, I think it's best we don't see each other again." She agreed. This lasted for a long time. I kept up contact, always sent her Christmas and birthday presents, but not for Mother's Day.

I do not want to give the wrong idea about my life—that I did not enjoy my childhood—because there were times when I did. But my life was certainly not the norm, nor was it what I used to call the "happy, carefree days of summer." We had enough food and enough of what it takes to live. I guess what I was missing, and did not know it, was enough understanding.

After Mama and Daddy divorced, Daddy was so upset he almost committed suicide. He stayed in Los Angeles for a while and managed an apartment building I owned, but he was very despondent. He moved back to the Northwest, where he felt comfortable, and worked in a restaurant in Longview, Washington. Eventually he bought the restaurant, enlarged it, and turned it into *the* place to eat in Longview. I think Daddy was happy then, feeding people, meeting people, and surrounding himself with friends. He remarried, a wonderful woman named Fran, who gave him a wonderful life. All of Longview closed down when Daddy died in 1972 of a stroke.

A town closed down for my Daddy, and I still remember his happy, smiling face at some time during the day, every day. I miss him even now.

Mama remarried also, twice. Right after the divorce, she was drinking a lot and living in a trailer in California when she met and married a Mr. Johnson. I don't even know his first name. This marriage didn't last long. I gave them a set of silver as a wedding present, which was a dumb thing to do, but that's what you gave for weddings in those days. I guess the silver disappeared with the marriage.

Mama's marriage to George Snow, however, lasted more than thirty some years, until he died. George was not well liked. He died after a short illness for reasons unrelated to his lack of popularity. Mama, a few years before, had wanted to leave him. She and I had a short discussion about it, but then she decided he was just the same as he had always been— miserable—so she stayed. I guess she decided it could be worse.

Last year Mama called to tell me she thought George "was on his way out," as she put it. I reminded her, "Be careful what you wish for or you might get it." Well, he was, and she called to give me the news. "Well, honey, George died. Of course, I'm not going to give him a funeral." "No, Mama," I said, "no one would come." "Yes," she agreed. "And besides it's so expensive. Three thousand dollars for the casket. I have no way to get out to select it, and you can't ask someone to drive you to do that. I can't drive. You know, my eyes are so bad. George never wanted to be cremated, so I had him cremated. Do you think I was wrong?"

"Well, you have to live with it, Mama," I said.

"The nicest lady came to the door the other day," she said. "Oh, the neighbors have been so nice, honey, and she told me about a water service, and it's only one hundred and fifty dollars."

"You mean the Neptune Society?"

"Yes, I guess so. They give you a rose, and you throw it over the side of a boat, they say a prayer, and you scatter the ashes on the water. Of course, I don't think I'll go because I've got to take the bus, and I'm just not up to it."

That's funny Mama. She finally got back at him. I guess for thirty plus years she did find some happiness. And I'm glad, I really am.

A few years ago, because of my cousin Barbara's nudging, I tried to patch up our differences. I called Mama and told her I wanted to see her, that I would fly to San Francisco and come to her house, or she could come to my hotel. She chose to come to me. We talked, had lunch, and talked some more. Finally I asked her, "Do you think our problem is jealousy?" She was quiet. I asked her again if she was jealous of me. She nodded her head—yes. "I guess so," she said.

That was all she said. Our big conversation was over, but it mattered. Maybe it was too late for us to go deeper. I just know our relationship changed after that. We talked in February, and the next Thanksgiving Mama came to my house, for the first time in many years. She had never *seen* my house. The children came, Mama's best friend, Peggy, came, too, and we all had a wonderful time (like a real family). The next May, when I was working in San Francisco in *I Do, I Do* with Howard Keel, I invited her to visit and we had a wonderful time again.

But then came September. I was in Seattle, still performing in *I Do, I Do*, when I received a note in handwriting I didn't recognize. It read: "In the audience, have the usher show me backstage," and it was signed "Mama." I thought it was a joke. There was a knock on the door; I opened it and it really *was* Mama. What a surprise. She was a little tipsy, but I was glad to see her. Glad and surprised, until I asked her how long she'd been in town. She'd been in town two weeks.

"Two weeks?" I was stunned. "Why didn't you call?"

"Oh, I was sure you were too busy to see me," she caustically answered.

I could feel anger rising and my stomach turning into knots.

Too busy to see her! Too busy! Our relationship hadn't changed after all. Why did she want to picture me like that? Why did she turn me into a daughter who wouldn't make time for her mother? Didn't she want to see *me*?

A few years ago, I was very unhappy, and I went to see a man recommended by my singing teacher. He wasn't a psychiatrist or psychologist, he was just . . . well, my singing teacher called him his "guru." I liked this man, George Falcon. I trusted him. We'd talk about my childhood, but I kept saying, "I can't remember it." "But it is there," he would say. "All of it is there." Finally he asked me if I wanted to be regressed. I wasn't sure, but I was game.

I know it sounds crazy, but I saw myself in the womb, crying and screaming, not wanting to come out. I did everything I could to stay there; I did not want to come out. I could see light and suddenly out I came—with a *POP!,* a thud. A thud, a scream, then a cry.

I also saw myself being suffocated with a pillow by my mother. It was as though I were a camera looking down on it all. I could even see the house, the bedroom, feel the stillness. I imagine I was about eight or nine. It was in the afternoon, kind of hot, so it must have been summertime because Portland doesn't get very hot. Mama came at me and held the pillow over my face. I struggled and screamed, and then she picked me up, and hugged me, and, finally realizing what she had done, rocked me and cried. All this was *very* hard for be to believe. I said to George, "Are you sure I didn't just see this in a movie?" He said, "Did you?" No, I don't remember seeing a movie like that—but did it *really* happen?

I started thinking, putting the pieces together. Mama's anger, her frustrations. Maybe I *wasn't* wanted. Maybe that was the something I felt was missing. I was getting older, Mama was getting older, and I had to find out. One night I was sitting at my desk and I dialed her number. We talked a bit, then I said quietly, "Mama, I want to ask you something." "Of course," she said. "Did you want me?" She didn't answer. I said again, "Did you want me?"

She answered hesitantly, "I didn't know *what* you were going to be."

"But did you want me?"

"It was the Depression," she said heatedly.

"But did you want me? Mama, did you want me?"

And Mama said, "No."

✱✱ 3 ✱✱

IN JUNE 1943 I finished eighth grade at Beaumont Elementary School. I wasn't looking forward to summer much, but I was elated to be entering Grant High School in September. That was the ultimate. I had a vision of boys and milk shakes, football games, cheerleaders, art books, school lunches, best friends, and dances. I was fourteen and aching to be ordinary. Grant High seemed to promise me a new life, a magical, ordinary life.

Before fall, however, came summer. I had a storybook notion of the Perfect Summer, summer as it *should* be: hammocks, playing kick the can under a streetlamp, walking in the country, going to a farm and seeing pigs and cows and collecting eggs, riding bicycles with other kids at dusk, hearing Mama call, "Time for dinner," children running, and running myself, to wonderful meals with homemade ice cream for dessert, or sitting in a canoe on a lake. Special vacations with Mama and Daddy. These things had never happened. It was a dream, a fantasy, a movie I'd seen or that book I'd read.

This particular summer, however, not long after school let out, Mama, Daddy, and I took a vacation—to *Hollywood*. That vacation changed my life, our lives, forever.

I remember we stayed at a terrible little hotel. It's still there, on Sunset Boulevard, a tiny, economical hotel across the street from what was then a bowling alley. I remember the sunshine and palm trees—I picture a small, brown-haired fourteen-year-old girl walking in that hot, dry, unfamiliar sunshine and staring at those shimmering palm trees, just like in a Dorothy Lamour movie. It looked like a movie set. Brighter and bigger than life. Even now I can recall that feeling when I see a palm tree, or oranges growing on trees!

In a funny way, that was the start of my life, that hot sun and those palm trees. I have other memories, of course, but this one is particularly sharp and clear.

I knew our Hollywood trip that summer wasn't just an ordinary vacation. I was supposed to appear on Janet Gaynor's *Hollywood Showcase: Stars Over Hollywood*, a famous radio talent show, but I was mostly excited about meeting Miss Gaynor and seeing the sights. According to a press clipping from that time, my "only interest was to see Hollywood and as many movie stars as possible" (a bit of an exaggeration). Singing on the radio didn't seem like too big a deal anymore—I was still doing two shows back home, but being at CBS in Hollywood with those radio stars, was. The president of KOIN in Portland, Charles Meyers, had arranged my appearance on *Stars Over Hollywood* with the help of my manager, Carl Werner. I even knew I'd sing my old standby, "Il Baccio," that's what every soprano sang in those days.

I remember walking along Sunset Boulevard on the morning of my performance, staring at palm trees and feeling very grown-up in my brown- and white-striped T-shirt, brown pleated gabardine slacks, and Wedgies. I still had a child's body, and a child's mind, and I was flat-chested, but I was aware of my new small breasts under the thin striped shirt. I was so happy that day. Daddy was with me. I'm not sure where Mama was. In my head I see Daddy and me walking proudly down Sunset Boulevard, hand in hand, framed by the palm trees, the eight or so blocks from the hotel to CBS. I had had my usual hot chocolate and toast that morning, cooked on our hot plate. (We had sneaked it in again, just like we did in Oakland.)

Visiting CBS was terribly exciting, maybe even more so

than going to MGM for the first time. Radio entertainers like Jack Benny, Edgar Bergen, George Burns, and Gracie Allen were big, big stars in those days, like television personalities are now. People would stand in line for hours to see them. For me, the radio stars were the most exciting people in the world.

I can still smell the linoleum on the floor of CBS. It had such a clean smell, not like the school linoleum. This was special, a professional, big-time smell. Almost as soon as we got there I remember meeting Meredith Willson, who much later composed *The Music Man*. I was so thrilled! I think he was conducting the station's orchestra. I remember standing in the hallway watching performers come and go, so busy and energetic—but my own performance I hardly remember at all.

I suppose I was nervous—of course I was nervous—*Stars Over Hollywood* was a talent competition and there were other contestants besides me. Did I want to win? Of course I wanted to win, that's why I was there. (But I didn't realize then how winning that contest would change my life.) I don't remember who the other contestants were or what they sang or did. I hardly remember my own aria. But I do remember the studio audience rising to its feet and cheering. Cheering for me. Kathy Lee Gifford told me not long ago that her mother was one of the contestants, too, and was glad I won.

The next thing that happened—well, a lot of things happened at once. People always talk about important events in their lives being like a dream. This really *was* like a dream. First—right after the show aired—Levis Green, a well-known agent with MCA (a major theatrical agency) called the station and wanted me to meet Louis B. Mayer at MGM the next day. Then Janet Gaynor, who was a friend of David O. Selznick, set up an appointment for me to meet *him*. So, before my heart had stopped pounding from all the applause, before I even realized where I was, I had auditions scheduled with *two* major movie producers, and I'd only been in Hollywood a couple of days! But I still didn't understand the importance of it.

I can remember my audition at MGM so clearly. I had already met Mr. Selznick that day, which was easy and pleasant, and then we had an appointment with L. B. Mayer.

I was wearing a chintz pinafore Mama had made, with bobby socks and white shoes. I was *terrified*, and so were Mama and Daddy, I now realize. The three of us, shy hicks who had never been anyplace before, eager tourists who confused Hollywood with Oakland, were now walking into Louis B. Mayer's office.

The walk seemed endless; Mayer's office seemed huge. I was in that office many times over the next decade, and each time it seemed smaller, the better I got to know him and the taller I got.

On this day, however, everything was gigantic: Mayer, who was actually a small man, the vast office, his enormous desk. Other important producers were there, too, sitting on both sides of the room. Joe Pasternak (who was later to produce several of my films), Arthur Freed, Jack Cummings, and other executives. The room was full of important men we didn't know. Mayer sat at the far end, behind his desk—I felt as if I were being presented to the king and his court. I stood by the side of the desk and sang, looking out at all those faces. Mr. Mayer's hair was white, what there was left of it. He wore g'asses and had a large, sharp nose, and was friendly but businesslike. I was so nervous I couldn't smile.

I had rehearsed before the big event with the pianist Arthur Rosenstein, who later became my teacher. He now took his place at the piano, and I took the usual singer's pose, hands clasped and poised, feet in fifth position. My parents moved off to a corner of the room, where Mama wrung her gloves. Daddy was nervous, too, but he could smile better than Mama or I. The singing part—"Il Baccio," of course, and "Summertime," I think, my favorite song then—was easier than smiling. I could always sing, but I couldn't always smile.

The king and his court were all very attentive; and they seemed to like me. Then Levis Green sent us back to our little hotel to wait. A few days later—without ever taking a screen test—I signed a seven-year contract with MGM, starting at $225 a week and going up to $1,250 a week. That was more than Daddy earned in two months; eventually I would be making $5,000 a week, more than Daddy earned in a year.

Selznick had me for one picture a year, but never exercised the option.

It was every teenage girl's wildest dream, and it was really happening to me. I should have been the happiest girl in the world! Well, I wasn't.

I really *didn't* want to sign that contract, even though obviously I'd never been offered such an opportunity, or so much money. I desperately wanted to go back home and go to Grant High. It sounds stupid now, but Grant High was more important to me than MGM. I'd convinced myself that high school would be different from grade school. This time I was going to get into the social swing of things; things *would* be different. And now, suddenly . . .

My parents said that signing with MGM was my decision. "If you don't like it," they told me, "you can change your mind in a couple of years and go home." It was all up to me. I was torn, really torn. I thought it was selfish of me to pass up such an opportunity; everyone would think I was crazy, and I couldn't disappoint my parents. I'm sure they thought I made the decision for me, but I really did it for them. Now, I don't want to sound like Pollyanna, but I knew it was *very* important to them, they had sacrificed so much. In a way, this was the best thing that had ever happened to them, and to me, too. I felt then—and I feel now—that if I hadn't accepted MGM's offer it would have destroyed Mama and Daddy sooner, and would have made their marriage even harder and more unhappy.

I cried when I finally signed the contract. Everyone assumed, of course, that they were tears of joy, but I knew they weren't and felt guilty for my feelings.

Crying, just like in those baby pictures. Oh, it's not that I was always unhappy—in fact, after a while, I began to accept where I was—it's just that I was so lonely. The performing, the singing and dancing, was pleasure. I loved that part. It was the rest of the time, the time off camera, the time with nothing to do, the time alone—it was everything else *but* the performing that made me feel so lost. I was horribly lonely those first few years in Hollywood. There was a gnawing, an emptiness in my stomach much of the time. I'd felt lonely before, but this was worse. I felt like a misfit, an impostor; like someone just playing a part. When I wasn't working or performing—I had no idea what to do with myself. When the cameras were turned off, "Jane Powell" disappeared, Suzanne disappeared. I had a glamorous job, what else could I possibly want? And I believed it. "Look how everyone envies what you do. What more could you want?" I guess I wanted it to be *my* desire, *my* dream, not somebody else's.

We went back to Portland for the rest of the summer to pack up the house and say good-bye. I still had some singing engagements, still had my local radio shows, but the rest of that summer is a blur. My scrapbook from that period is crammed with letters from Portland officials—from the mayor on down to the chairman of the Hood River County War Savings Committee—congratulating me on my sudden success. "Dear Suzanne," wrote Mayor Earl Riley, "wherever destiny takes you, Portland will be watching with interest and enthusiasm." Wherever destiny takes you! If only he knew how much I didn't want to go.

I remember that Daddy bought a used convertible for the trip back to Hollywood. I guess he felt we deserved to drive a flashy convertible now that Hollywood was ours. We drove down from Oregon in September. It was fun—with the top down, but we all got terrible sunburns. We pulled up in front of MCA, the talent agency that had discovered me, and parked. There we were, people from Oregon, sunburned and dusty, with all our suitcases in the backseat. "Well, here we are." Daddy told Levis Green. Levis looked confused. The agency didn't know what to do with us. All they were supposed to do was take care of the contract—they'd done that. They weren't obliged to find us a place to live, but we thought *everything* had been taken care of!

They must have been amazed at our innocence, or ignorance, but they did manage to get a reservation at a local hotel, a dingy little establishment. It was most colorful. Lots of ladies! Soon after that, we found a small walk-up apartment, in Beverly Hills, not the posh part where *real* movie stars lived, but it was convenient and near MGM. We stayed there for about a year; then we rented Donald Meek's house. (He was a great character actor in many films—*You Can't Take It with You* for one—and I was thrilled to be living in his home, though we never met him.) The house was really cute, with two bedrooms, a garden in the back, and furnished in chintz.

After a few years in California, we finally bought our own place in the San Fernando Valley, a ranch-style house with a small pool. Daddy had always liked Early American furniture, and that's what we got. I had a salmon-pink canopy bed covered with flowered material, and a new kidney-shaped dressing table with a peach and white organdy skirt that Mama made. The bed was so high that I had to use a footstool to climb into it (like Scarlett O'Hara, I thought).

But that was later, after Suzanne became Jane. Now we had just arrived in Hollywood. I think my parents were as lost as I was. Daddy went to work at the Samuel Goldwyn studios. He got a union card and became an electrician on the set. Then he took over the coffee wagon for the crew and stars. "The best coffee wagon of them all," they all said. Eventually he left that and opened his own doughnut and ice cream shop. I'd work for him on Friday and Saturday nights, even when I was earning a top salary and neither of us had to sell doughnuts. It was his place, and there Daddy and I would sling out those hamburgers and hot fudge sundaes. I don't think Mama ever worked there.

We had a big opening for Daddy's store, Paul's Malt Shop, on Sunset Boulevard. My Hollywood friends showed up for the fan-magazine photographers and Daddy, Roddy McDowall, Elizabeth Taylor, Jerry Courtland, Darryl Hickman, Ann Blyth, and many others were there. Ann is so pretty, gentle, strong, religious. Every inch a lady. I always felt like a loudmouth when I was with her.

The shop was plastered with pictures of various stars and me (especially me), which was very embarrassing, and there were klieg lights, too, that night. It was really just an ordinary little doughnut shop, but this was *Hollywood* and Daddy's night. Everyone ate themselves silly, and the hot fudge flowed like wine. Elizabeth popped her skirt button, and I broke out in pimples.

I was terrified my old friends in Portland would think I'd become a snob. My girlfriends from home would write me letters about basketball games, dances, and boyfriends and all the fun they were having. I'd read the letters and cry, then I would write back and tell them only about singing lessons and school. I rarely mentioned anyone I had met or seen, anyone they might have heard of; I never mentioned the movies I was starring in, I was too afraid they'd think I was bragging. I guess my letters must have been *very* dull, while their letters seemed exciting to me.

I wonder now why I was overly afraid of telling them about myself. The worry of being thought of as stuck-up was always prominent in my life, and I worried that performing had somehow made me "different." I realize now that I blocked out a lot of the wonderful things that were happening to me because I was afraid of being special. "Nothing much happening here," I would write my friends—when in fact a whole new world was happening.

I started working almost as soon as we got to Hollywood, which was very unusual, I was told. I arrived in September, and all the mothers, stage mothers just like the ones back in the Oakland days, ready to pounce, said, "She won't do a picture for ages." In fact, Roddy McDowall's mother, Wynn, said, "Oh, Suzanne won't do a movie for a year or two." But in November, two months after we arrived—the mothers were aghast—I started working on my first picture, *Song of the Open Road*. I still hadn't had a screen test and I was the *star* of the movie.

In those days, the studio had a lot of contract players, young people, and often they didn't do much at first; they would just be part of the "atmosphere" and studio. The difference with me was that I sang. I know now the studio was looking for another Deanna Durbin when it hired me because Deanna had left movies by then. I had always loved her and wanted to meet her, and I still do. In fact, Joe Pasternak, who became my producer at MGM, had been Deanna's producer.

Song of the Open Road wasn't an MGM movie; I was loaned out to United Artists and the producer, Charles R. Rogers.

(Rogers, too, had been one of Deanna Durbin's first producers)
It was an amazing potpourri of actors and performers—Charlie
McCarthy and Edgar Bergen, W. C. Fields, Bonita Granville,
Jackie Moran, and Sammy Kaye and his orchestra. I felt as if
I'd closed my eyes and walked into a movie—and I had!

I had never had an acting lesson in my life, but that didn't
seem to worry anyone. Later, back at MGM, I did have an
acting coach, Lillian Burns, who taught most of the MGM
stars. The one thing she taught me was not to wrinkle my
forehead when I talked. For my first two movies, though (I was
loaned out again for the second one, *Delightfully Dangerous*),
I had no training at all. I had no idea what I was doing.

In a way, it's easier to be a child performer; you have
nothing to unlearn. It's when you get older that inhibitions set
in, that it becomes hard. I never had to play a character; they
just told me to be myself. If I was supposed to be sad, I thought
about something sad. I just did what I was told, as always.

When I look at my old movies now, I'm amazed at how
comfortable I seem in those roles. They said I was a natural,
but I just played myself—I guess that's as natural as you can
get.

Even the dialogue was often just me talking naturally. At
first, I'd go home and learn all my lines, word for word, but
then I'd come back to work and find the whole scene had
been changed. So after a while I stopped memorizing lines
verbatim. Because I was always playing girls my own age, and
the directors always wanted the characters to sound like me,
my vocabulary, comments, exclamations, or whatever, would
work their way into the script. Eventually something would go
down on paper, but the actual words were as likely to be mine
as the writer's. These days I try to say the lines the way they
are written, but it's very difficult for me. All my training has
not been so exact.

I was concentrating so intensely during that first film that I
hardly noticed what was going on around me, but some part of
my mind stayed alert in spite of itself. I realized this a couple
of years ago when I attended the opening of a Broadway play.
I was waiting for the curtain to go up when a woman came over

and sat next to me. "Jane," she said, "you don't know me, but . . ." I said, "Yes, I do, you're Susan Simon." She was the daughter of Sylvan Simon, the director of *Song of the Open Road*, and I hadn't seen her since she was ten years old! How I remembered her, how her name came to me, I will never know. I hardly remember her being on the set, but she told me she had always been there, following me around. "You were so nice to me," she said. "You were so friendly." Even though I don't remember this, we are great friends now and I'm glad she never forgot.

That's how I feel about my past. Maybe everyone's past is like that; it sneaks up on you, like a half-familiar face in a darkened theater.

In *Song of the Open Road*, which was released in 1944, I played Hollywood's idea of "myself"—a rich but lonely child movie star who runs away from home to join a band of teenage crop pickers. This wholesome group of young people doesn't like me at first, but eventually I save the day, and an orange crop to boot, by enlisting the help of my Hollywood friends, Edgar Bergen, Sammy Kaye, and W.C. Fields. Isn't that a plot for you?

A "typical poor-little-rich-girl tale," said *Variety;* but "Miss Powell has a fine voice." "Jane Powell, called a second Deanna Durbin, does sing remarkably well, in a high, clear, true voice," said the New York *Daily News*; but *Song of the Open Road* is just too naive in theme and haphazard in presentation for adults to take, comfortably." The *New York World-Telegram* added: "The film, which also opened on D-Day, drew a 'D' in movie reviewers' report cards, while its star drew an 'A' for her effort."

I *loved* making that movie; it was all new and exciting. They kept me so busy I didn't know if the film was good or bad; the question never even occurred to me.

I remember we locationed in Azusa (A to Z in the USA), California, and in Palm Springs. We stayed in a hotel in Palm Springs. We shot scenes in a date grove and rode bicycles through it. Imagine riding bicycles in a date grove! The sunshine was wonderful, the hotel was wonderful, the pool was wonderful. Flowers had fallen into it and it looked so romantic, I thought. Everything looked romantic, like a movie set.

This was during World War II and there wasn't much glitz in Hollywood, but I didn't know the difference. Instead of two or three klieg lights, they'd use one. But it all looked great to me.

They didn't touch my brown hair for that movie, but they slathered my face with heavy makeup, greasepaint really. In those days you used so much makeup, your face would crack. Even if you were a child and didn't have wrinkles, by the end of the day you did. I never had the usual adolescent skin problems until I started wearing the makeup. Then I began giving myself facials with almond oil and oatmeal soap to get the makeup out of my pores. Of course, our lips were painted big and red. That was the style—huge red lips. Nothing was done with subtlety.

I wore a blond wig for the first part of the picture because my character had supposedly run away from home and dyed her hair. I remember the flies drove me crazy when I wore it. I'd be doing my schoolwork and they would be buzzing all around my head. It was the spirit gum, the glue that held down the wig, they liked. I felt like the character in Dick Tracy, the one with flies buzzing around his toupee. Finally they had to bandage my head with gauze so the flies wouldn't get in my eyes and give me welts.

For me, even the flies were a new event. Here was this young girl, fourteen years old, who had never worn a wig, never been to Hollywood, never been in a movie, meeting all these people she had heard about for years. So many "nevers." It was all so thrilling and frightening and unreal. No wonder I felt as if I didn't belong; yet here I was the star of the show. I didn't dare wonder if I was good enough.

It was exciting—but lonely, too. I don't remember any of the other actors talking to me much—maybe because I was still in school—but one of the specialty dancers did talk to me, Stan Catron. He became my boyfriend later, and I wrote to him while he was in the army. Bonita Granville, who played the head crop picker's sweetheart, was quite a bit older than I, in her twenties, I think, and had been acting for years. She was a real "child star" and might have been a bit unhappy that a younger newcomer was getting so much attention. Jackie Moran, her boyfriend in the film, had also been around for a while, and I was a very *young* fourteen; there wasn't much we could say to each other. I felt like a real outcast, as if I shouldn't be there, but there I was.

I was much too afraid to talk to W. C. Fields, who had a small cameo role in the film. He had a drinking problem, which was known to everyone but me. Once, we were on location, and one of the shots they had to get after lunch took place in a truck with Mr. Fields. But every day, after lunch, Fields was nowhere to be found. The director, Sylvan Simon, realized that the only way he'd get the shot was to lure Fields into the truck early in the day and *leave* him there during lunch hour. And that's what Simon did. He got Fields to go into the truck, made him comfortable, called lunch, and took the ladder away! Fields fussed and fumed a bit and soon fell asleep. We had one scene together in the whole film, and he ad-libbed it all. I was at a loss for words.

Because of that movie—actually, to publicize it—I became Charlie McCarthy's girlfriend on the radio. I was his love for about a year, appearing on *The Chase and Sanborn Hour*.

Charlie wasn't every fourteen-year-old girl's idea of a good time, but he was quite appropriate for *this* Girl Next Door. No one had to worry he might get fresh.

While I was on the show, Edgar invited my parents and me to his home to see Charlie's bedroom—a completely furnished room and bath! It was as though a real person lived there. Charlie even had his own toothbrush, scaled to size. It was fascinating, and weird at the same time.

Edgar married late in life, but when he did he chose a lovely, gracious woman, Frances, Candice's mother. We had the same dressmaker for years, so our paths crossed often. I often wondered how she coped with that living—but hardly breathing—person in the downstairs room.

When the film came out, I went on my first publicity tour—my first trip east—twenty-six cities in forty-six days. We went everywhere by train because of the war; there were no planes. Mama was with me, and a publicity man from the studio, and we took trains and trains and more trains. There are photographs of me in Grand Central Station in New York, sitting on my luggage with my legs crossed, a typical pose. I wore a powder-blue suit and a little hat that was a kind of beret with a silver hummingbird pin on it. They always took provocative pictures of female movie stars sitting on luggage— but, of course, I was fifteen years old and anything but a sex symbol. Provocative? No.

Everywhere we went, there were photographers and I always had to smile, and I hated it. I always felt I had a big, ugly mouth. My teeth were crooked on the bottom, and I would try to cover my mouth with my hand so they wouldn't show. In fact, from certain angles it looked like I was missing a tooth, so the studio gave me a little cap I could glue on during filming which I kept losing and almost swallowing. Because I was a young girl, and they wanted that image, they didn't try to make me glamorous—but it would have been very difficult, anyway.

So there I was, crossing my legs in Manhattan and smiling for the flashbulbs less than a year after we had left Portland. Mama was smiling, too. I was fast becoming famous.

A strange thing happened just before I started making *Song of the Open Road*, just before Suzanne disappeared. Someone from the studio called one night when I was ironing and asked, "Hello, is this Jane Powell?" And I answered, "No, I'm afraid you have the wrong number." The voice on the other end said, "No I don't, honey. That's your new name. *Your* name is Jane now." That was it. What a way to get a name.

I've been asked, what was it like? Was it traumatic getting a completely new name? Thinking back, to me it seemed like the normal chain of events. They told me "Suzanne" was too long for the marquee, and of course no one could pronounce Burce for some reason; so probably it would be changed. But "Jane"? That was the name of the girl in the movie. To this day, people still think I'm Dick Powell's wife, William Powell's daughter, or Eleanor Powell's sister. I always wanted my name to be Cheryl.

** 4 **

IT WAS EXCITING making films, singing and dancing, meeting stars, but . . . Oh, I'm not complaining; I've had opportunities most people only dream of, I know it, but as a teenager I often felt more obligation than excitement. During my first four years in Hollywood, from the September I arrived at age fourteen until the November I was eighteen, I never had a vacation. Everyone was depending on me. Mama and Daddy, the producers of all my movies (I had made six by 1948, the year I turned nineteen), my fans. Sometimes I just wanted to run away from it all, like the character I played in *Song of the Open Road*.

I didn't think about vacations. I assumed it was normal to work all the time. I thought I had no choice; it was my job, and everyone said I was lucky. (I *was* lucky, I kept telling myself.) My job was an all-year-long thing; there was nothing I could do about it. I used to do my Christmas shopping in January in case I was too busy in December. In fact, I still shop early. I'm getting a little more flexible now, but I'm still afraid of not having it all done by Christmas. I guess I'm leery of running out of time.

For so long, time was precious, and it's hard to slow down even now, when I can. All those years in Hollywood I wore a

watch to bed, I was so afraid of being late. How many
teenagers sleep with a watch? It's crazy when you think about
it, but I did.

When I look back on those years now, it seems as if I was
always running, always working, always busy. Even when I
wasn't filming, or rushing to classes at MGM's Little Red
Schoolhouse, or doing my homework, I was working
somewhere—taking lessons, doing publicity, or singing at
charity performances. I was always asked to do benefits
because I could sing. The child stars who only acted never
seemed to be invited. They were lucky. I have eaten so many
creamed chicken lunches I should have feathers. I'd do the Red
Cross, or the Braille Institute, the Kiwanis again, or the
Chamber of Commerce again, the Jewish Home for the
Aged—I really got benefited out! I'd have to practice first, get
together with the pianist, worry about what to wear, then
finally do the benefit itself. It all took a lot of time. And on
Easter Sunday, many Easter Sundays, I'd sing at Easter sunrise
services at Forest Lawn or the Hollywood Bowl. I'd just go
where they told me, open my mouth, and sing. I didn't feel
what I was doing, for that particular cause, was important. I
felt removed, not a participant, just there.

I performed at the Jewish Home for the Aged for many years
because L. B. Mayer's sister, Ida Mayer Cummings—who was
also the mother of Jack Cummings, the producer of *Seven
Brides for Seven Brothers*—was very active at the home. It was
wonderful of her to do that charity work, but she was a bit of
a tyrant about it, I'm afraid. If you said you couldn't perform,
oh my! She'd get so upset. I hardly ever said no. She was a
very sweet lady, but she had me confused with Margaret
O'Brien. "I just loved your little pigtails. Why did you cut
them off?" she would ask. I'd just smile. I never wore pigtails.

I've been looking through dusty old copies of contracts I
saved from those years and it absolutely amazes me to see how
busy I was. I shuffle the fading pages, sneeze as the dust is
stirred, stare at our signatures, over and over: Suzanne Burce
("professionally known as Jane Powell"); Paul E. Burce
(known as "Father"); Eileen Burce (or "Mother"). Over and

over, my name in girlish flourishes. Daddy's large, bold signature, studded with sweeping capitals. Mama's cramped writing, much smaller than either of ours, over and over and over . . .

I sang on Hedda Hopper's radio show, on Frank Sinatra's program, on *Stars Over Hollywood, Maxwell House Coffee Time, Lux Radio Theater, The Railroad Hour,* among others. I recorded *Hansel and Gretel* for the Columbia Recording Corporation; appeared at the San Bernardino National Orange Show; starred in *The Student Prince* at the Greek Theatre in Los Angeles; sang in the Hollywood Bowl on I Am an American Day (May 16, 1948); performed at a benefit for the Portland Symphony Orchestra back in my hometown; at a luncheon for the Society of Motion Picture Engineers; with the Philharmonic Orchestra in Kansas City, Missouri; and at the dedication of the Variety Boys' Clubhouse in Van Nuys, California. I sang at the "Movie Star" baseball games at Wrigley Field, did a benefit for the Motion Picture Relief Fund, and so many other things. I even sang at the inauguration ball for President Harry S. Truman on January 20, 1949. I was on a vaudeville tour, appearing with a movie that I was not in. We were in Washington at the time I finished my seventh performance of the day and rushed over to the ball to sing. I did get to meet our president, but by that time of night, everything was a blur. I can't remember what he said or even what I thought of him.

No wonder I felt I was running. No wonder I slept with a watch.

And all this wasn't even my real work. My real work was making movies. My real work was being the "girl next door."

It was demanding—and making the movie was just the beginning. Many times when a film was completed I went on tour for publicity, travel to different cities with Mama, smile at flashbulbs, sing at press luncheons, always talking and singing. And for many years when I was "on hiatus"—which meant I wasn't working for the studio—I'd go to movie theaters around the country doing a vaudeville act. I'd play Loew's theaters because they showed MGM movies; I did New

York, Buffalo, Cleveland, Chicago, Pittsburgh—the circuit. And I *hated* it. Oh, how I hated it! I wanted to be home. I think I was the only person who was glad when vaudeville died.

Not many people remember vaudeville today. It was exhausting. We would do seven or eight shows a day, seven days a week. First, the movie started at nine-thirty or ten in the morning, followed by the vaudeville show, then the movie again, then the show again, and on and on, until ten or eleven at night. I'd be the headliner, and there would be a comic, possibly, a dance team, a big band, a dog act or acrobats or all of them. All the big orchestras with bandleaders like Skitch Henderson, did it. Skitch and I have been friends for years and have worked together many times. He had the orchestra on *The Perry Como Show,* and is now the conductor of the New York Pops at Carnegie Hall. We worked together there recently. (I finally made it.) The big bands were very popular in those days. Sometimes the stage would rise and the orchestras would rise up out of the floor. It was spectacular. They would play a set and then, possibly, the Step Brothers or the Nicholas Brothers, great dance teams, took over. The the comic, more orchestra again, and then I'd come on. I played with Buck and Bubbles, Joey Adams, Shep Fields and His Rippling Rhythm—many vaudeville greats. I hated it! Not them. It was all so confining, so isolating.

I recall the first time I brought my act to New York. I was sixteen, and I was playing the Capitol Theater on Broadway—it's not there anymore. The theater was big, cold, and imposing. My fifteen-minute act included numbers like "The Donkey Serenade," "Kiss in the dark," and "Les Filles de Cadiz," with "Summertime" as an encore. *Variety* liked it. "Miss Powell," they said, "registered as a likable singer in her first Broadway personal appearance." But "Miss Powell" herself *didn't* like it.

The studio had put Mama and me in an empty apartment on Central Park West. It had little furniture, no telephone, no food or restaurant. It was like being marooned on a strange island—we *were* marooned on a strange island. We soon moved to a hotel, a real fleabag. We didn't know where to go, but it was close to the theater, and we could walk there, saving taxi fare. One day years later, while I was performing on Broadway in *Irene*, between the matinee and evening performances I was lying down and happened to glance out of my dressing room window, and there it was—that same hotel. Oh, the memories came flashing back that day. I thought, *Look where I am today.*

Then there would be lines around the block, people trying to get into the theater, pushing and pulling for autographs. I'd spend the whole day and night at the theater—I even had my meals brought in. There was no time, or way, to go outside. There was never any time.

I guess I could have said no to all this, but I never said no, I didn't know how. The studio made money from the shows; my agent, who set them up, made money, and in a way Mama and Daddy made money . . . I was a kid; I just did it.

I try to remember now how I felt about all that money; I didn't understand it. I never saw it, so it wasn't real to me. I started earning a lot right away, and shortly I was making five thousand dollars a week, an unimaginable fortune in those days (when a Manhattan apartment might rent for fifty dollars a month). Mama gave me a ten-dollar-a-week allowance, which bought gas for the car I got when I was seventeen, and my lunch. She made most of my clothes and I would borrow some gowns from the studio for big do's. I would have loved to go shopping, but Mama said I didn't need anything. I didn't know anything about money, and no one was about to tell me.

I certainly didn't think we—or I—were rich. We lived in a modest house, bought with my money, which I didn't know. I had a very modest allowance, to say the least. Daddy was a working man, and I helped out at his malt shop. We didn't even have a maid. Where the money went I don't know, but I never got any of it, not even later. When I married at twenty-one, I left everything I owned with my parents. I didn't take anything but my clothes—I even left my bed behind. I felt my possessions would be a kind of insurance policy for them, protection so I wouldn't have to take care of them in later life.

It didn't work that way. Soon after my marriage, Mama

divorced Daddy, and as far as I know she kept all the money. It didn't even help her as much as it could have; I don't think she ever invested in anything worthwhile, if at all. We were all so ignorant, we didn't understand money. I was twenty-one-going-on-twelve, and Mama and Daddy weren't much better.

Even though the famous "Coogan law" was in effect, named for child star Jackie Coogan who earned millions of dollars for his mother and stepfather but never saw any of it himself, money seemed to melt away. The law, passed in 1939, required parents to set aside some portion of a minor's earnings, up to one half, and save it. There were lots of loopholes, however, and parents or guardians seemed to find them. Besides, in my case, loopholes didn't matter; I voluntarily gave all my money to Mama and Daddy.

I remember standing in the receiving line at my first wedding, and a woman, who had been handling the taxes for my parents, came up to me and said, "I always get money back for you, you always get a rebate." And I said, "Oh, do I? That's wonderful." I didn't even know what a rebate was; I barely knew what taxes were. Well, that year I was hit with $25,000 in back taxes. Of course, I didn't have any money; I had nothing in reserve. I'd left it all with my parents. I was really very stupid. And I've been audited ever since.

Even today, I'm very careful, very frugal. I always know exactly what bills I'm writing checks for. I'm very conservative about what I buy. My biggest expense is shoes—I love shoes and they're very hard to find because of my size, 3½ or 4. They're the one thing I'm extravagant about.

As soon as I finished the publicity tour for *Song of the Open Road,* I began work on my second film, *Delightfully Dangerous.* Apparently MGM was still waiting to find the perfect vehicle for its new "find." (It worked out well for the studio, loaning me out; I got all my training on someone else's time! By the time I came back to MGM, at least I knew camera left from camera right.) Ralph Bellamy, now a good friend, was in *Delightfully Dangerous.* He has said time and time again, "That was the worst movie I have ever made." And I'm inclined to agree. (One critic called it "a mild trifle at best" and *The New York Times* found the film "more dangerous than delightful.") When the movie came out in 1945, the reviews were generally negative, although very kind to me.

I didn't know it wasn't a good film. I had a good time working in it. I was playing Constance Moore's younger sister, Cheryl (I finally got to be a Cheryl), who was too innocent to realize her big sister worked as a bubble dancer. I got to wear a tutu and pretend I was on a tightrope, that's what I remember most. But I knew that Morton Gould, the conductor, who was also in the movie was miserable the whole time we were filming. He'd never been in a movie before and he was terribly uncomfortable, very self-conscious, and wanted to go back to New York. We reminisced about it not long ago. He's a very funny man, dry and witty. I was also extremely impressed with Arthur Treacher, who played Bellamy's butler. Treacher played everybody's butler and had been in films since the year one. I was always fascinated by character actors, even back in Portland when I barely knew their names, but I knew his.

Character actors, I think, are the real stars, the ones who hold a movie together, the ones whose names people rarely remember. They're the people who work hard all their lives and never see their pictures on the covers of magazines. They won't be telling their Cinderella story for someone to read in a movie magazine; theirs is more a tale of *The Little Engine That Could*. I'm not saying I'd want to trade places with them, not if I'm honest. But these men and women, the real faces among the tinsel, have my genuine respect and I'm sure I speak for the rest of my peers.

My life as an MGM "star" (I find that a very difficult word to use, "star." I wonder why?) actually started with the third movie, *Holiday in Mexico,* a big Technicolor extravaganza (my first two films were in black and white). *Holiday in Mexico* was to introduce me to the world (again); the great thing from my point of view was that it introduced me to my costar, Roddy McDowall, still one of my dearest friends. Roddy's been like a brother to me. And since I have no real brother, he's *better* than second best. He's a good, good friend.

Roddy played my sweetheart in *Holiday in Mexico*, a lightweight romantic comedy set in Mexico City. Afterward, he gave me a photograph inscribed TO MY FIRST SCREEN FLAME. (We were never an item, just good friends from the very beginning.) Walter Pidgeon, playing an American ambassador to Mexico, was my father in the film. I was so in awe of him, and he was so attentive to the little girl from Portland. Just the way he ate a grape fascinated me. I first met him at a birthday party for Louis B. Mayer and—I don't remember if this really happened—after I supposedly sang "Happy Birthday," Walter (Mr. Pidgeon) rushed over to L. B. Mayer and said, "That girl is terrific. Who is she?" And Mayer is supposedly to have answered, "She's your daughter." I adored him, but I could never bring myself to call him Walter. It was just "Yes, Mr. Pidgeon," "I'm ready, Mr. Pidgeon." He was such a charismatic person.

I was that way with everybody, really. I never became close to any of the adult stars I worked with because I was too shy, too scared. Except for Roddy, I didn't make many close friends in Hollywood. I would have loved to have a circle of really close friends—but I was a loner. I never felt like an insider, never. Maybe everyone else thought I was, but I thought I was the least important person around. Even in real life I felt I was acting; I kept waiting for someone to unmask me.

You see, I always wanted to be liked by everybody. That's not so unusual. I just carried it too far for too long. I just never made waves. I was so insecure and afraid of rejection, I thought whatever I said was not important and wouldn't interest anybody, so I never got into any lengthy conversations. I was sure I couldn't keep up. I felt dumb and uninformed. I'm not sure if I *really* wasn't accepted or if I just felt that way, but it doesn't matter much anymore. One time, soon after I got started in Hollywood, my parents and I were invited to a "wrap party" for one of Shirley Temple's movies, *Since You Went Away*. We had arrived in Hollywood just weeks before. A wrap party is an end-of-picture party for everyone involved with a film, from the actors and director to the cameraman, electricians, prop people, everyone on the set. Everyone stands around complimenting each other on how great he or she was, recounting the film's gossip, and the usual "we-must-get-together-soons" flow as freely as the alcohol. But soon everyone forgets and goes on to the next epic. These parties can be very glamorous, with glorious food, elegant decorations and people, so you can imagine how intimidating (and thrilling) such an event seemed to my parents and me, brand-new arrivals, still stunned by Hollywood.

This particular party was held at David Selznick's studio, in the commissary (the dining room), and my parents and I stood off in a corner and tried to make conversation among ourselves. We didn't know *anyone*. Before we went we worried about what to wear. What can you possibly wear to such an unprecedented event? Your best party clothes? Of course—party dress, hat, gloves. (We were wrong. We looked like the hicks we were.) We drove through the gates and felt terribly important when the guard checked our names on a list and beckoned us through. Then we opened the door to the commissary and were hit by an intoxicating wave of noise.

The room, much smaller than MGM's commissary, was filled with colorless mahogany booths—but the stars were all there, anything but colorless. Joseph Cotten, Jennifer Jones, Myrna Loy, Robert Walker, and Shirley Temple herself, were all walking about and talking, talking like regular people. But they were talking only to each other. Selznick's publicity man met us at the door and told us to make ourselves comfortable. Comfortable? We stood in our stiff, unfashionable party clothes and tried to blend into the scenery. We tried not to look too much like tourists overcome with awe.

I could see people looking at us, wondering who we were, *what* we were. Unfortunately, I caught Shirley Temple's reaction. I glanced across the room at her and saw she was imitating me, copying my gestures and exaggerating them, acting like a phony opera singer. She was singing "Il Baccio," I was sure. I guess someone had asked her, "Who is *that*?" and she said something like "The new singer on the block." When she caught my eye, she stopped, embarrassed. She pretended it hadn't happened, and so did I.

But I'll never forget the sight of her mocking me. It made my heart stop for a moment, I was embarrassed for us both. Mama, Daddy, and I left the party as soon as possible and drove home to our little apartment. We were very quiet on the way home. I think that was the start of my feeling that people were laughing at or belittling me. It increased my sense of isolation, of never fitting in. I know we were never invited into the inner circle, my parents and I. Or maybe we were, but just didn't go.

The people I really felt closest to when I was working were the crew. The other actors and actresses intimidated me, especially since they were so much older and more experienced than I. The crew seemed more like real people, people I was used to back home, people I could feel comfortable with. There was a wonderful man on my first movie, *Song of the Open Road*, the head electrician, Bob Jones. My parents and I became good friends with him and his family; we had more in common with them than with the other crowd.

Bob gave me a lovely identification bracelet which he'd had made. It was sort of a joke, because when you go onto the lot you always have to show the guard some ID. I didn't have any and was always asked for it by the guard. I always had to explain why I was there. It was a silver oval bracelet, beautifully inscribed, and I saved it for years. But recently my jewelry was stolen and that went, too. I was heartbroken. It can never be replaced, but I have the memory.

The crew on the film *Delightfully Dangerous* gave me a collie puppy, for my birthday. I know I cried buckets over that. It's funny what seems important now, so many years and changes later.

According to *Life* (September 9, 1946)—which posed me in a one-piece bathing suit, sticking out my small chest and pointing my toes into the sand—"The young soprano thus sought out by fame and flashbulb is a cheerful, thoroughly nice, slightly undersized teenager."

The producer of *Holiday in Mexico*, Joe Pasternak, who went on to produce most of my movies, remarks about me,

"There is no difference between her and other little girls. She doesn't even look like an actress." That was for sure!

He's an old man now, not well I am told, and I'm sorry about that. I thought of him the way I thought of L. B. Mayer, like a father, like a protector. But that was a long time ago.

Joe Pasternak was more or less assigned to me, and I to him, the way Judy Garland was to Arthur Freed. We used to be good friends; I would go to his house for dinner and swimming, and visit his family. His children were babies at the time. I really thought we were friends. I was his daughter, he would say; I was the one he wanted to pat on the head instead of on the behind. It's true, however, one time I found out he was giving a good-bye party for my friend David Rose and didn't invite me. I thought it was strange, but I just assumed it was one of those things. One of those things that hurt for a while but eventually you let them pass. But much later, years later, I heard a story that did more than hurt for a while.

Word came to me through the grapevine that some man had asked Pasternak about getting a date with me. And Pasternak said, "Oh, Jane Powell, she's the easiest lay in town." And then he added, "She's so easy even my son Peter has had her." I was so hurt, so *shocked*. I felt betrayed. If I was easy, nobody knew it, including me! I hadn't been around at *all*. I was so naïve and innocent, I used to joke that I was the only mother-of-three in Hollywood who was still a virgin. If a fellow asked me to dinner, I thought I should marry him.

I called Joe on the phone and told him what I had heard and, of course, he denied it. What else could he do? But from then on I couldn't think of him as a protector or as a father figure again.

I first worked with Pasternak on *Holiday in Mexico*, a lavish, frothy musical directed by George Sidney. I got to fall in love with Roddy McDowall *and* with José Iturbi, who was a grandfather at the time. One big number was "Ave Maria," sung on a very large stage, supposedly the Hollywood Bowl, where I performed many times. One critic described the scene as "a Eucharistic Congress staged by Billy Rose." Everybody thinks that because of the movies I did, like *Holiday in Mexico*,

Nancy Goes to Rio, or *Luxury Liner*, I was always on location, but in fact the *only* location I went on was for *Song of the Open Road*, when we traveled to Azusa and Palm Springs. Everything else was filmed at the studio. In fact, if the set was big and expensive it would be used again and again. Nobody knew the difference—it would be dressed up with plants, new colors and new props and new people, and it would look completely different.

Whenever I went onto the set I could smell the special paint used on the floors. (It seems I'm always smelling floors, doesn't it?) It was new, just dry; that sharp burning smell is still fresh in my mind today. The arc lights would click, click, sputter, psssst, click when they were warming up. (They were extremely hot, particularly for Technicolor movies.)

I was mostly in pictures set in sunny climates, except for *Seven Brides for Seven Brothers*. If you'll notice, many musicals—or TV shows like *The Love Boat*—are set in sunny climates. It makes everybody look better, and more romantic, and it makes everybody happy, particularly audiences who live in cold climates. I know it sounds silly, but it's true.

My hair was still brown in *Holiday in Mexico*, but it was getting lighter; and it kept getting blonder and blonder as the years went on. The studio started bleaching it just a little because my mousy brown hair was hard to photograph—but pretty soon no one remembered it had ever been brown.

So "Jane Powell," soon to be blond, made her first big Technicolor movie, became a Metro-Goldwyn-Mayer star, and posed on the cover of *Life* magazine when she was seventeen. The little brown-haired Portland girl was fast disappearing.

I'll tell you how I felt then. Not like Cinderella and not like Jane and not even like Suzanne anymore. Everyone said I was wholesome and sweet and darling, but I felt I was an ordinary person doing an unusual job. Who *was* this Jane Powell, The Girl Next Door? I wasn't really The Girl Next Door, and I didn't feel like a movie star, either. I didn't know what I was. I just felt a real Girl Next Door had a better time.

She knew more than I did, dated more than I did, had more friends than I did. She had a mother and a father who were loving to each other. She went to football games, had pajama parties, flirted with boys, ate lunch with girls, saw movies with boys and girls, drank sodas in the drugstore. She took physical-education classes, ate in the school cafeteria, worried about shaving her legs and wearing silk stockings. I was not that person. I didn't have that life.

The Girl Next Door had such simplicity—and that *was* me without all the rest. But I kept that simplicity for much too long. For thirty-five or forty years, I was a sweet young thing. "Stay as sweet as you are," they said, "and never change."

I had happy times. My exterior was not a complete fraud. But there were times when I was alone and no one saw me. That was when the emotions crept in and the actress stepped out. I have always been able to turn these feelings off . . . quickly . . . these somber, lonely feelings, so no one ever knew I had them. And then again I buried them for so long from myself. I was afraid of letting down, of letting the feelings out, for fear of not presenting myself as Peter Pan, that person who was told, "Never change, stay as sweet as you are." I carried this image far too long. I remained a juvenile way past my prime, with no help from anyone to change it. I was afraid I would disappoint someone.

Who was that Girl Next Door? Not me. I felt like a fly on the wall looking down on it all, an observer. I was still in Portland, Oregon, kind of lost, maybe sitting on a rock.

"STAY AS SWEET as you are." "Don't change." "Stay the girl next door." "Don't grow up." *"Don't change."*

I was good at that. If the studio wanted me to wear a pink dress and I wanted a yellow one, I wore pink; I didn't even think of arguing. If they told me to smile, I smiled. If they told me to sing, I sang. We were all very sheltered, the child stars of those days, because if we got into any trouble the whole world would know about it. The studio warned us, and our parents warned us: "Look what happened to so-and-so. It had better not happen to you!" It was like being trapped inside a television set you couldn't shut off. The world kept watching.

I was so painfully careful, so afraid of disappointing everyone (*anyone*), so desperately eager to please. I stayed as blah as I was at fourteen! After a while I felt like the oldest teenager in the world.

By the time I wanted to change—by the time I was *determined* to change—I didn't know how to. I no longer knew what part of that sweet, innocent Girl Next Door was real. She (I?) wasn't allowed to make decisions, to show anger, to think. I had the oddest sense of detachment sometimes, as if I were in the audience staring at myself. I didn't know how to play; instead, I *watched* myself playing. I was removed. *Do I look right?* I wondered. *Here I am laughing,* I thought. *Am I doing it right?* I was playing a part. I don't know who was the first Girl Next Door in Hollywood, but Doris Day and I carried the banner together for years. However, I continued running with it long after she did. She got smart. I always envied people who had a burning desire and worked toward a goal to *be* or *do* something they wanted. My life wasn't that way. For a long time I didn't dare to dream. I *lived* a dream, but it wasn't mine.

Since I was The Girl Next Door, how could I think about sex? I was Miss Goody Two-Shoes, so how could I know any dirty words or dirty stories? Or even listen to such things! I was never supposed to change; so how could I grow? I was like a child sent out of the room whenever the conversation got steamy. Physically I was growing. Mentally I was not.

I was a young fourteen, a young fifteen, a young seventeen, a young eighteen when I worked on my fourth movie, *Three Daring Daughters* (in which Jeanette MacDonald played my mom), and a young nineteen by the time *Luxury Liner* and *A Date with Judy* appeared (both in 1948). I got sacks of letters from other teenagers asking advice about dating and romance, but I barely knew how to act with a boy. (The studio answered the letters for me!) For a while I even had an advice column in a fan magazine, telling teenage girls not to wear too much makeup and teenage boys how to ask for a date, and answering letters. But I haven't the slightest idea who wrote it. I know I didn't. How could I?

Dear Jane:

I am a girl of 14 and I go with a boy who is 18. He is really swell. My mother approves and thinks a lot of him. He says he likes me too. A year ago he went with another girl. A few of my girlfriends don't like me, and think that girl is wonderful. They are doing their best to break us up so this boy will go back to the other girl. He doesn't want to. Should I give him up or just not pay any attention to the other girls and continue to go with this boy?

D. E., Yukon, Fla.

Don't you think you're a little too young to be dating—and so seriously? But since your mother approves, why should you consider giving up this boy? You and he don't want to; you'd just be catering to those other girls who apparently are jealous. I'm surprised you call them friends. Their behavior doesn't indicate that they are.

JANE POWELL

It's odd reading those letters now; it was odd reading them then. (I'd had less social experience than many of my correspondents.) It's no wonder I felt detached. All those eager strangers poured their hearts out to "Jane Powell" and "Jane Powell" replied, offering delightfully sensible, wholesome, wise advice. The idea that I would "write" an advice column embarrassed me. Who was I to say that a girl should leave her boyfriend? I wanted one myself.

I always liked boys—even in the first grade. Boys were great—but I was boy-crazy only in my mind. I thought you could get pregnant if you merely sat next to a boy. And if you really kissed a boy, French-kissed him, whatever that meant, you would get pregnant for *sure*.

I was very frightened of sex. I didn't know what sex was; I didn't understand the feelings. And I couldn't get any answers from Mama. I learned not to ask her about anything "dirty"; dirty had something to do with sex. The words "sleeping together" were *very* dirty; they conjured up a disgusting picture in my mind. I'd heard the expression at school back home, but I wasn't sure what it meant. Something to do with sex, I knew. Something repulsive.

I had a little kitten and she slept with me. And after hearing those words, "sleeping together," I was petrified. I agonized for weeks, then finally decided to approach Mama. "Mama," I said hesitantly, nervously, "if you slept with a cat, could you have kittens?" She looked nervous, perplexed. "I don't think so."

The kitten never slept under the covers again.

The fear started when I was very young, about eight. There were several older girls living at the Banbury Cross—I was the baby in the group. One girl's mother worked, so that apartment was empty all day, and the gang, three of them, would take me there whenever they could. Even now, I get chills writing about it. They would push me onto the couch, take down my panties, and do something with a Coca-Cola bottle and a candle. What they did exactly I don't remember. I've blocked that out, but I can imagine that I was their guinea pig, their experiment, their amusement, and I was frightened of them.

I knew what we did was "dirty." I know I was frightened. And I felt guilty. Would this awful thing be happening to me if I weren't bad? Children often feel that way. If only I could have told Mama or anyone. If only I could have talked to somebody about those girls who came at me with Coke bottles and candles. If only I could have shared the secret—but I couldn't. I could never, never speak about anything so dirty. Nice girls didn't talk about or do dirty things.

One night, I was lying awake on my fold-out couch in the living room; Mama and Daddy, I assumed, were asleep in the bedroom. Suddenly a toilet flushed. Mama and Daddy tiptoed in; Mama whispered, "She didn't hear a thing." My heart was pounding. Why did I feel that something bad had happened? Did I connect it to "sex" and that empty apartment upstairs? I still remember my anxiety, my strong sense that something was wrong. Every night after that, I slept very fitfully.

For years, I hated the sound of a toilet flushing, particularly in the middle of the night. I had always felt it was because we lived in apartments and the noise would wake the neighbors up, but now I know it wasn't.

Oh, I was innocent, but my confused fear of anything "dirty" didn't stop me from having intense crushes on boys. I would pick out a little boy I thought was the cutest one and pretend he was my boyfriend—I liked that word, "boyfriend." It was sweet and friendly. Maybe I just wanted a brother. Maybe I just wanted a friend.

I remember my early crushes, the valentines edged in lace,

cutting hearts out of stiff red paper and gluing them on paper doilies. I still smell the paste—like wintergreen.

Jerry Fay, my first heartthrob in fourth grade, had fallen out of an apple tree and broken his arm. It was withered and paralyzed, permanently twisted into an awkward position, but he rode a bicycle better than anyone else, flying like the wind, not even touching the handlebars. I can still see him with his long neck, widely spaced teeth, and the stocking cap he never took off. I think the mother in me was touched by the twisted arm, and by the boy on the wild bicycle.

Then Bill McComber, so cute and shy, short with dark hair, quite a catch. I knew he liked me, but in eighth grade, boys weren't suppose to show it, and he certainly didn't. I saw him again a few years ago. He is still cute. And then Jack Smith—he did show it—Jack shoveled sawdust for our furnace in the basement one summer while I baked him brownies. That was my biggest Portland romance. It was a brief one. Before the brownies had cooled, it seemed, I was living in Hollywood.

Stan Catron, who had been in *Song of the Open Road,* and I were fond of each other for several years, but right after that film he went into the army. I do remember coming to New York once and meeting his parents. I was very excited about it, but he was very nervous. He kept saying, "That's the Bronx, they live in the Bronx." I said, "So?" Again he said, "The Bronx!" This meant nothing to me, but what he was trying to tell me was that he was Jewish. I said, "I know that. It doesn't make any difference to me. Should it?" He was relieved. He must have agonized over that for months.

And I did like kissing and necking (not that I did much of it), but I was terrified of "going too far," as they said, back then and I wasn't really sure what "going too far" meant. Stan used to kiss me on the cheek—and nothing any lower than the mouth! But I felt guilty.

I felt guilty if I was late, guilty if my work didn't go perfectly. I felt guilty all the time. I'm really very lucky that none of my dates ever tried to take advantage of me. In fact, they usually sat down patiently and explained sex to me, but I was always skeptical. Mama had always told me not to trust a man. "They'll tell you one thing," she would say, "but it won't be the truth."

I recently talked to David Holt, a former child star I dated for a while. He'd tried to tell me about sex, I remember, but I didn't believe him either. David was a real cool character. He'd been going with Marilyn Maxwell before me, so he was quite sophisticated. I thought I was in love with him, but he treated me like dirt, standing me up, arriving late. However, he never took advantage of me. "I was afraid to touch you, Jane," he said not long ago, "because you were so sweet and innocent. I'd never met anybody that innocent before."

I *was* innocent, all right, but so much innocence isn't a blessing. I loved it when someone would discuss things with me like David. I was desperate for someone to talk to.

I envy women who have women friends they grew up with, went to school and college with. Those are lasting friendships. I envy the worlds they explored together, the experiences and feelings they shared. I envy their *conversations*. That part of my life is vacant.

I had no real peers in Hollywood. I was the only one in my class at the Little Red Schoolhouse at Metro, so it was hard to meet people, as you can imagine. My best friends in those days were boys or young men, and there are certain things you simply *don't* talk about to males.

I didn't know how I was supposed to feel about anything. I had no basis for comparison: Was I supposed to feel that emotion? Was there something wrong with me? I had no one to giggle with. The only guidelines I ever had came from the movies. And of course you didn't see much of anything in the movies then. I never had a conversation that went "What was it like? What did he like? Did you do it?" I didn't know those words. The kinds of things I wanted to know you couldn't find in a book. There were novels like *Fanny Hill* and *Lady Chatterley's Lover,* which I read in later years, but they were just novels—they weren't real. As for my parents, they were the ones who taught me all the noes. If there were any yeses, they didn't mention them, their own relationship was so stressful. I didn't get a very positive picture of marital love.

I'll never be a child again, and I feel a real sadness and loss. Today parents ask me, if you had it to do over, would you? Do you think my child should go into show business? I answer, no. No, for a couple of reasons. If the talent is there, then usually the time will be there. But what is most important is your childhood—you can never replace that.

So many things were forbidden when I was young. So many things were "dirty"—there were so many no-no's: Don't look at nude statues. Don't touch anyone else's body; don't touch your own body in the "wrong" places. It never occurred to me to ask why. Did everyone memorize the same rules? My teenage isolation greatly hindered my later sexual and emotional growth: I'd better not do anything wrong, or I wouldn't be the sweet little girl everyone loved.

I was naïve not only about sex but about *everything*. One spring I was singing in Fort Worth, Texas, for a charity affair. My agent, Jules Sharr, was with me. After the performance, someone asked me if I would like to see Amon Carter's Remingtons. Mr. Carter was one of the wealthiest men in Texas and a supporter of the charity.

"Remingtons! Why, of course," I said. "I'd be thrilled."

I can see it now. As I stepped into the limo, I turned to Julie and asked, "Why would anyone want to collect typewriters?" "I don't know," Julie answered.

Two babes out of Toyland. What a surprise it was to see those priceless paintings and sculptures.

During a movie when the camera panned discreetly away from two lovers on a beach beneath the palm trees, I never had any idea what the couple was doing. *Oh, what a pretty picture*, I would think. *Oh, look at the lovely sunset*. It wasn't until I was in my late twenties, or maybe early thirties, that I realized just what those lovers were up to.

When I married my first husband, Geary Anthony Steffen, Jr., I was still a virgin. We had known each other for two years and had fooled around a bit, but we never actually slept together; I was twenty years old, but I went into marriage like a child would read a storybook—I imagined children, cookies, and a white picket fence. Geary was a sportsman, Sonja

Henie's ice skating partner. I was so impressed, and I thought I was in love. Even after I got married, my head was full of questions. I assumed I would get pregnant right away, as soon as we "did it." But we did it, and I didn't. Of course, I was sure that something was wrong with me.

It's very hard when you've been told all your life that sex is dirty. "Don't touch that." "Don't do *that*." Or, "You know what *they're* like." Funny, isn't it? I was taught to say yes to everything, but sex.

How difficult it is to be young. And when I was a girl I seemed to be in a constant state of embarrassment. I was embarrassed at having to excuse myself to go to the bathroom (everyone would *know*). Once, I put off going and had the accident you have nightmares about. This was back in Portland. I'd been invited to a play by an adorable boy. He was a grade or two older, so I was thrilled. It wasn't really a date—a girl who lived in our apartment building had come along, too—but at least I had been noticed enough to have been invited. We sat in the school auditorium on hard wooden chairs with slats. I sat tensely, trying to look nonchalant, while this adorable boy kept looking at me. But I desperately had to go to the bathroom.

I didn't know how to excuse myself. I'd never been out with a boy before. Just as I was getting up enough nerve to leave, saying I had to get a drink of water, the lights went out and I had to sit down. Then the inevitable happened: a puddle under the chair and a very wet dress. I rushed off, hoping my dress would dry if I stood in front of a radiator, but of course it didn't. Luckily I had a sweater with me, so I tied it around my waist with the back hanging down over my rear end. It was the best I could do.

Times, when I was dating, I thought of myself as being "in love"—with Stan Catron, with David Holt, with Tommy Batten, then with Geary. (And, of course, each time I got married, I thought I was in love forever.) Tommy was my biggest romance before Geary; I was about seventeen when we met. He was doing a movie with Wallace Beery (who played my father in *A Date with Judy*), but Tommy was really a college student. He was studying to be a dentist at the University of Southern California, but he didn't want to be a dentist. He wanted to be a singer, and he is today.

He had no money and a car that was always breaking down; I thought that was great. The college scene was thrilling; I'd always wanted to go to college. We went to fraternity parties; we were "pinned"; I was "serenaded." At last I was The Girl Next Door in real life, and I loved it.

I loved *it*. I was in love with love. With Geary, I was in love with the white picket fence, and diapers on the line. With Tommy, I loved playing the part of college sweetheart, riding around in his junky old car because that's what a college sweetheart would do. When I try to remember him now, I see scenes from our courtship, like movie scenes: Here I am climbing gracefully into his car, dressed in a full skirt with all the petticoats. And he is asking me to "go steady." Here we are kissing. And what did I *feel*? Butterflies! But is that love?

It's hard for me to say, "I love you." I'm never sure I mean what other people mean. "Love" is a word, but do I *do* it right? I know that I love, but do I love as much as the next person? Could it be that I love more? Many times I feel inadequate and confused when I hear people talk about love and how deeply they care. I get embarrassed and I don't know why. I want to give it so badly. But am I doing it right?

✳✳ 6 ✳✳

By the time I was seventeen or so, Hollywood was my way of life.

My way of life! I was glad when this foreign existence began to feel almost natural and I *almost* fitted in. My daily routine became . . . routine, even ordinary, a sort of "doesn't everyone?" life.

Hollywood was, and is, in the fantasy business, but up close you can see the props. And I loved them! The prop department of MGM was like a museum, a glorious collection of real and unreal, of every period, every style you could imagine, and some you could *never* imagine. If they didn't have something, they found it. If they couldn't find it, they made it, and made it accurate in every detail. It was the same with the costumes: They were authentic down to the underwear! Even our petticoats were of the finest materials. Ribbons and lace, silk or chiffon, crystal pleats. Such *care* was taken in those days.

In *Seven Brides for Seven Brothers,* the girls' dresses were supposed to be made of quilts. It would have been easy to whip up dresses that *looked* like quilts—but instead the designer, Walter Plunkett, went to the Salvation Army and found old quilts, and turned them into marvelous, authentic dresses for all the brides.

If you needed a sofa, you went to the prop department; if you needed a whole house, or a whole country, you went to Lot 2 or Lot 3, the location lots. Andy Hardy's house was built on one of those lots. You could find lakes and trees, sidewalks and lawns and cozy suburban homes, a bandstand, a bridge, whatever you wanted; you could walk right in. It reminded me of those fairy-tale villages they build for children. The bridge I walked on in *Royal Wedding* was also used in *Waterloo Bridge, Mrs. Miniver,* and who knows how many more films. And I defy you to recognize it—each time it was transformed, like magic.

All the costumes for MGM movies—women's and men's—were stored in the wardrobe department, and I would have a field day rummaging through them. It was Grandma's attic, dress-up time, a child's fantasy. And I'd always *loved* dressing up. I remember being thrilled poring through those racks of clothes, a rainbow of colors, and feeling the taffetas, velvets, and satins. My costumes, of course, were designed for The Girl Next Door. To this day, people still comment on the dresses I wore in *A Date with Judy* or my formal gown in *Holiday in Mexico.*

Long after I stopped designing clothes for my paper dolls, other little girls were cutting me out of their paper-doll books and taking me to the ball in a paper dress created by the designer Helen Rose. Imagine being a paper doll, a child's toy, being part of someone else's private game. It's a nice feeling.

Clothes were so important to me in those days. I guess they were my personal props. They had to be just right; they had to create the fantasy—the one I starred in, and the one I lived. I had many, many costume fittings, but I never minded: Eventually the magic would appear. The seamstresses, those magnificent ladies, would be down on their knees in their black or print dresses, pincushions strapped to their wrists, measuring and pinning. They were usually gray-haired and sweet, accommodating, smiling. I'd stand on a pedestal, in front of four or five mirrors, twirling, showing the pretty petticoats, maybe singing a bit of a song from the movie or doing a couple of dance steps to see how the dress moved. And those wonderful seamstresses would somehow transform a sketch and bits of cloth into something phantasmagoric.

Helen Rose was the designer who created most of my things. She was dear and talented, a great friend. She designed my first wedding dress, and also Elizabeth Taylor's first. When Helen originally came to the studio, she went around in a nondescript black dress, with her slip showing and her hair pulled up in an unflattering knot. She didn't care anything about designing a wardrobe for herself. According to MGM legend, someone introduced her one day to L. B. Mayer. "This is our new designer." He took one look and ordered her to fix herself up or be fired. And she did, but her heart wasn't in it.

On the other hand, Irene, who did my costumes in *Holiday in Mexico,* was a genuine beauty. She was tall with lovely hair, and she loved clothes. Her color sense was impeccable. She created a wonderful greenish-blue color. Technicolor green, I called it. I loved it. To me, it will always be Irene green. Even her fingernail polish was hers alone. It was pink with a bit of blue in it; to me at sixteen, it was gorgeous, so *special*. She didn't stay long at the studio after *Holiday in Mexico,* and I missed her beauty.

Everyday life: How do you imagine a movie studio? Tinsel and glitter and glamorous stars? Fun and work? Well, it was all of those.

In some ways, MGM was like a small town. My singing lessons were upstairs in a large room over one of the sound stages, and I can remember looking out the window at the street below, at the bustling crowds, the trucks and cars and props being lugged from one set to another. They looked smaller from up there. Judy Garland might be walking by, talking in her usual animated, nervous way. Clark Gable might be strolling along, deep in conversation. Or I'd see Greer Garson, a lovely lady with a marvelous sense of humor, her red hair glowing in the sun. Or Esther Williams, Mickey Rooney, Lana Turner, June Allyson, extras in costume, messengers going someplace, just like in the movies. And this was my everyday life.

June Allyson was new, like me, but much less shy. As soon

as she arrived at the studio, it seemed, she became one of the group. I never did, even after I'd been there for years. The only place I was comfortable was at Roddy McDowall's. Thank God for Roddy, my dear, sweet friend—I don't know what I would have done without Sunday afternoons at his home. Especially those first few years.

Every Sunday, Roddy's house was a gathering place for all us Hollywood kids. His mother, Wynn, liked and wanted her children—Roddy and Virginia—close to her, so she would invite all their friends, her friends, every Sunday—it was a big open house. Everyone, it seemed, was there—Ricardo Montalban, Elizabeth Taylor, Darryl Hickman, Ann Blyth. People came and went all afternoon; we'd swim, play badminton, dance to records, have dinner, go home about nine or ten o'clock.

Wynn was a difficult mother for Roddy and his sister, Virginia, but I thought she was wonderful. She was warm and friendly, outgoing and confident. She was intelligent, and I loved being around her.

I loved Wynn, but later, after I married Geary, I realized it was terribly important for Roddy to get away from home. I told him, "You've got to get out of town and get away from your mother. That's the only way you'll survive." Wynn had been very good to me, but I could sense what she was doing to Roddy. She was destroying him as a man, as a person, and as a talent. The whole family revolved around Wynn; everybody was under her thumb. Every time the family didn't do what she wanted, she would feign a heart attack. Roddy was torn—he didn't want to hurt her. But he had to get away. I, at least, was married, but I believe now that I had married to escape my parents and their unhappiness. It was Roddy's turn now to escape.

In retrospect, I think Wynn was really a classic stage mother. Mama may have been tyrannical with Daddy and me, but she was shy around everyone else; you never saw her pushing me forward in any way. (Elizabeth Taylor's mother, Sarah, was different; she would nudge Elizabeth and say, "Honey, take a glass of water to the director." Elizabeth would squirm with embarrassment.) Wynn knew everybody's name and what they did and how they would help Roddy—she studied the scene.

I was so happy when Roddy left L.A., even though I missed him terribly. He says now I helped him make that decision, but he really did it himself.

On those Sunday afternoons at Roddy's, I liked being with the other kids, even though I still felt shy. I still couldn't say hello to a star, a name; I had no sense that I was one, too. *Why would they want to be friends with me?* I would think. I heard later that the others felt the same as I did.

Even though I enjoyed the work, and being busy, it always seemed to be dark when the workday started, dark and cold, despite its being sunny California. And it's no wonder, with those early morning—five-thirty A.M.!—makeup calls. The women envied the men because they didn't have hairdos and makeup sessions to contend with. It's hard to imagine those days when today blow-drying is all people know how to do. When I was young, a single hair and makeup job might take three hours or more. And we were supposed to be on the set by eight or eight-thirty, in costume, lines learned, ready to go. I'd stay up late, studying intensely, learning my part; then I'd crawl into bed with my wristwatch ticking away in my ear. My whole life was geared around time; I always wanted to know what time it was. I was famous for being punctual, was always being complimented for my promptness, so I knew I'd better keep doing it! I used to have nightmares about being late.

How chilly those mornings were! When the body makeup girl came by and slathered me all over with a cold, clammy sponge smelling of sea breeze, it always gave me a jolt. My skin still cringes at the memory. Everyone always hated the body makeup lady. It didn't matter who she was—we hated her. We'd see her coming with that sponge, coming to slap on the pancake—and we shuddered. One of them always wore fuchsia, so we called her "Fuschsia-Bell." Was she bothered by our complaints? No!

I was given a permanent dressing room after a few years, but I hardly ever used it—there wasn't time. All the women were in one section—Lana, and Esther, and Judy—and the men were in another. Nothing was coed in those days. Of course, the stories I heard suggested otherwise; but there was none of that coed stuff for me!

Being on the set was always a pleasure; I loved the costumes, the sets, the people, the hot, bright lights. The lights were intensely hot, and if you had on a tight outfit or did a strenuous dance number, they could be real killers. But there was something terribly exciting when those lights came on, and the director called, "Action!" Everyone and anyone came to life and sparkled, as if a switch had been pulled. Like windup toys, we started clicking—it was thrilling, every time, to me.

Life on the back lots: cameras and dressing rooms, lunch tables, lights. Sometimes barking dogs would follow us as we hurried from our dressing rooms to the set. Out there, the assistant director would be calling into his microphone, "Everyone on the set who is in this shot. Everyone on the set!" Most often that just meant extras, because the rest of us would be off somewhere rehearsing our scenes or, in my case, going to school.

When we were shooting outdoors, musical numbers would often pose special problems: High heels would get caught in the grass when we danced. Bugs would go down our throats when we sang—hazards that were unique to musicals.

I studied singing at the studio with Arthur Rosentein, MGM's vocal coach for operatic or classical singers. Rosie was a dear, but unfortunately he knew nothing about teaching singing. (I've had bad luck with voice coaches most of my life.) He'd been an accompanist for one of the leading sopranos of her day, but he was not a teacher. The studio was not aware of this, I'm sure. Neither was I. I studied with him for five years and all I ever learned to do was smile.

"Just smile, honey, and everything will come out all right." That's what Rosie would tell me. I followed this advice for years before I realized I didn't know anything about singing. Of course, the smile did make me photograph better, and I guess that was all that mattered to the studio. Later I had Jeanette MacDonald's teacher, who had a theory I still don't understand. "Concentration on vitalization," she would say. I was supposed to hold my thumb under my chin, press hard, and feel some muscle—but I never found it. I also had to feel the teacher's muscle. I hated that. She was very old and her neck was like a turkey's. It upset my stomach.

My next teacher, whom I got from Kathryn Grayson, had only one piece of advice: "Just break your bra straps, Janie." Unfortunately, I didn't wear a bra! So that period didn't last very long. There were other teachers, probably five or more. They all had theories, and all their theories confused me. But not one ever taught me how to breathe properly. I guess they thought I knew, but I didn't.

The pop singers at MGM had completely different coaches. I worked with them occasionally and I think that is what started my singing problems. I was a soprano—so I always got the high notes. I love to sing ballads and the blues, but I rarely got to do them. I hardly ever got a chance to introduce a song, either. I always wanted to have a song on the Hit Parade. But because I was a soprano, I did remakes of Jeanette MacDonald, Deanna Durbin, Gloria Jean—anything with a high note. They even tried to give me a Nelson Eddy number once—"Stout-Hearted Men." When I did *Two Weeks with Love,* for instance, I sang "My Hero." But a relative newcomer, Debbie Reynolds, got to sing "Aba Daba Honeymoon." You can guess which one of the two made the Hit Parade!

The biggest thrill for me back then—and it still is—was listening to an orchestration being played for the first time. It gave me goose bumps to hear a song I had been working on for weeks played by thirty-five or forty fantastic musicians. The recording studio for all the underscoring and songs for the movies was right on the lot. I used to love to go by and listen to the orchestra, but I was a basket case recording myself. I was afraid to make a mistake. I thought the musicians were perfect; I felt I had to be perfect, too. But you didn't have to be perfect—you could record your number or even one note over and over—but I found that horribly embarrassing. Luckily, I rarely needed many takes. I was so anxious, desperate to get it right and get out.

Hearing my recording played back was excruciating. I heard only the mistakes. When it was finally over, I would gasp in relief. I always recorded early in the morning—partly because I was an early riser and had more energy then, but also to get the ordeal over with.

When other stars came by the set to watch us work, I'd get terribly nervous. I wanted to be so good. "They probably aren't even looking at you," I'd tell myself over and over, but it didn't help. I loved watching other performers, particularly legends like Spencer Tracy and Katharine Hepburn; I felt privileged and thrilled to be in their presence, almost as if I were in a church. The Tracy-Hepburn sets were usually closed, but I'd manage to get in.

For years we worked a six-day week. According to the law, child actors were only allowed to work eight hours a day and had to go to school at least three of those hours. That meant we were constantly rushing; as soon as there was a break in the shooting, we had to hurry off to school. And as soon as they needed us again on the set, we'd be called back. Our time was measured. Someone was always waiting. It was difficult to find time even to go to the bathroom.

Bathrooms were a big deal—they were never on the set. Sometimes they were just next door, sometimes three or four stages away. I had chronic constipation because I didn't feel I could take the time. And everywhere I went, I ran so I wouldn't be late.

In between everything else, I had acting lessons with MGM's drama coach, Lillian Burns. I don't think I got much out of these lessons, though—Lillian was always talking on the phone and seemed to stay on the phone for hours.

Because my eight or so hours included makeup, school, work, and lunch, I had to run. I'd get to the makeup department, and that would take two hours, or maybe an hour and a half if I was lucky. This was before television and the pace was very different, *much* more leisurely. I'd wash my own hair, but they'd put it up in rollers and sit me under the dryer. And the makeup itself took forever. We wore heavier makeup then.

Film today is more sophisticated. Now everything can be done in an hour or less.

In the old days, we'd rehearse our dance numbers for three weeks or more. For *The Andy Williams Show,* or TV specials with Red Skelton, Dinah Shore, Jimmy Durante, Judy Garland, with as many or more dance numbers, we only rehearsed for five days. In summer stock you have six days to put *The King and I* or *The Sound of Music* on its feet before you open, and if you're not ready, you go on anyway.

Working with those great stars was a joy. Red Skelton, one of the sweetest men I know, always had everyone in stitches. His prebroadcast dress rehearsals on a semiclosed set were unbelievably raunchy—in fact, downright vulgar—but they were *funny.* People in the know would clamor to be in the audience for those rehearsals.

Jimmy Durante had such energy, even in his later years. Until he died, Jimmy secretly supported his old show-business cronies financially. He never forgot them.

After makeup, at eight or eight-thirty, we'd start shooting what was set up, and then I'd go to school. We had to stay in school at least fifteen minutes at a time; that was the rule. Some days I'd make up my entire three hours in fifteen-minute segments (a strange, confusing sort of education!). If we had time for more than fifteen minutes, that was great. (Bathroom time, of course, was not included.) And if four o'clock came around and I hadn't gotten my three hours in, the production would have to stop, at least as far as my scenes were concerned, so I could finish school. That was the Los Angeles school system—they didn't care if the movie got made or not, but they certainly cared about those three hours.

Other days, when I wasn't needed on the set, I'd go to the famous Little Red Schoolhouse. Every day, Monday to Friday, nine to twelve. We were all together, kids of all ages—but even there I was the only student in my grade. I'd be doing my work; Elizabeth Taylor would do hers; Skippy Homeier and Darryl Hickman would be doing their work, too. But we were in different grades.

The Little Red Schoolhouse wasn't red, but it had a red tile roof. The architecture was Spanish, with graceful arches, and the walls were stucco and painted Navajo white; the school was like a little bungalow. Just inside the doorway, I remember, there was a kitchen, which doubled as a nursery for the very small children, and there was another room for the first to fourth grades.

Elizabeth, who's a couple of years younger, and I became friends. (Later she was a bridesmaid at my first wedding, and then I was a bridesmaid at *hers*. I'm certainly glad we stopped that bridesmaid stuff—it could have become a full-time career!) Judy Garland, Lana Turner, and Mickey Rooney also went there, but before I arrived. Margaret O'Brien and Dean Stockwell, the little kids, were in a room by themselves—the kindergarten–first grade area. The rest of us worked in the big room. Some days the school would be crowded; other times it was almost empty.

Our principal and head teacher was Mary McDonald, "Miss McDonald"—a legend among MGM youngsters. I really didn't like her. I thought she was mean and cold, but I never said anything because I thought everyone else was crazy about her. Well, here it is years later, and I just found out *lots* of us didn't like her!

Miss McDonald didn't do much teaching—she was more of an organizer, the principal—but she was always there to greet us. Coldly. We didn't always have the same teacher, either; and we never had the schoolhouse teacher on the set. The teachers were generally good; they all came from the Los Angeles public school system. Every year we had to go down to L.A. for exams and all those normal high school rituals. I'd say our education was merely adequate. We covered the basics, but there was no time for frills, and I regret that.

We had reading, writing, and 'rithmetic, and that's about it. No gymnasium, none of the extras I'd hoped to get at Grant High, back in Portland. I took mathematics—the *same* mathematics—over and over again for four years because I was so terrible at it. I never got to geometry. It was embarrassing . . . but they couldn't let me fail. This would have been more embarrassing—for them.

I guess I learned enough, and I did graduate from high school. We *had* to graduate from a public school—that was the rule—we were actually supposed to show up in cap and gown, and pick up our diplomas, at Uni High, University High School. I was afraid everyone would think I was stuck-up if I didn't go to graduation—my old anxiety—so I went, but it was dreadful. I didn't know a soul there and hadn't even met one person until graduation. They all stared, and I'm sure they talked behind my back.

I was miserable those few hours at Uni High. But I felt uncomfortable even at the MGM commissary. There, important stars usually went right to a table. Everyone else waited in line. Tables were reserved for particular departments—there was a publicity table, for instance—and occasionally for particular stars. Or you could just walk in and join some friends or take an empty chair. No one in my category stood in line—but I did.

I knew I wasn't supposed to be in line, or I sort of knew. But again I didn't want anyone to think I was putting on airs. Sometimes the hostess would see me and say, "Oh Jane, come in and sit here." I felt embarrassed if she singled me out—embarrassed but happy at the same time. It's nice to be recognized, but I was always afraid of stepping on someone's toes.

The commissary was noisy and busy, particularly between noon and one-thirty. Extras in costumes would stare at the star tables enviously, while waitresses—many of whom had been there for years—brought us our favorite dishes. L. B. Mayer had his own dining room within the commissary, and everyone watched avidly to see whom he had in tow. As soon as his door closed, all the watchers would start to speculate. "What are they up to? Do you think so-and-so's in trouble? Did you hear about so-and-so's new deal?" I rarely knew anyone who walked into that room. I was afraid of power, and that was a powerful room. You could feel it. You could smell it.

I sat wherever they seated me. One time Clark Gable came over to my table, leaned over my chair, and said, "Hiya, Janie girl." I just stared at him. I couldn't remember his name.

Another time I sat next to Marjorie Main, who played Ma Kettle in several movies. She was a wonderful lady, something of a hypochondriac, and a bit eccentric. When I sat down, I saw she was wearing white gloves. *Dirty* white gloves. I said hello, and she nodded, sort of. She didn't want to breathe the air I was breathing. She was too afraid of germs and many times she wore a surgical mask. I asked her, "Miss Main, please pass the salt." She picked up the salt shaker in her dirty white gloves and handed it to me. I finally couldn't stand it anymore. I asked her why she wore white gloves to eat her sandwich. "Afraid of germs," she said, "afraid of germs."

Miss Main also liked to sleep in her Cadillac convertible. She'd never had one before, and I guess she was afraid someone was going to steal it. She also wanted a glamour sitting—the kind of photo session Lana Turner used to have— lying on a bearskin rug, sexy negligée, long wavy hair. She got the sitting, but somehow she didn't look much like Lana—but she thought she did.

There were always new starlets or contract players in the commissary, coming or going. They came and went so fast it was almost impossible to remember their names. (Many times their names changed anyway!) I felt sad when their options were not picked up; they had hoped for so much. But the studio system was a good one. MGM was very astute about talent. It's much harder for young actors struggling today without any protection or guidance—and without funds to take lessons and buy clothes, publicity, a manager, everything needed to further a career. I was lucky. I wouldn't have had the life I'm sharing with you if it hadn't been for the studio system.

Am I lucky? Was the Little Red Schoolhouse better than Grant High? I still regret missing the normal teenage life, the feelings I suffocated. But I'm grateful for the opportunities I've had. If I'd stayed in Portland I might have continued singing; a couple of friends I still write to sing in the choir and maybe I would have, too. We would have raised our children together, been closer, talked over the back fence, but I do think my world would have been narrower.

There's still a lot of Portland in me, but I couldn't move back. That was then.

Everyday life? We all live it, in Hollywood or Portland or pulling weeds in Connecticut. The trick is to live it and appreciate it. And I think I'm finally beginning to learn how.

⁑ 7 ⁑

I HAD LOTS of movie daddies. Lots of mamas, too: I was everyone's little girl. My real daddy may have been off in his malt shop making up doughnuts and chocolate shakes, but on film, someone a bit more glamorous—maybe Walter Pidgeon or George Brent—was hugging his on-screen daughter. My real mama was watching and waiting nearby, but Ann Sothern or Jeanette MacDonald was even closer, beside me under the lights. I had more parents than anyone needed. But I still didn't have enough family.

However, a family was being created. A different kind of family, a family of strangers, of unknown friends.

Almost every day someone, somewhere, stops me and says something so dear and sincere:

You are a joy to see . . .
You give me faith . . .
I've loved you since . . .
If you only knew what you meant to me growing up . . .

Most of them say God bless you. It is wonderful to be a nice part of someone's life. If I had stayed in Portland, I'm sure I would never have been so lucky. This seems to be happening more and more. True, I am getting older, and so are they, and I'm still around to remind them of then and now—but they care enough to remember and tell me. Isn't that nice?

The career that was started and nurtured by my parents, and that happened to take off with luck and talent, is finally mine. I no longer feel like a fly on the wall, observing and hoping to survive. I'm alive and part of anything I care to be, and now I can choose the things I want to do. Not bad! I never expected to keep working as long as I have. I never expected my popularity to last. I never expected people to remember me. But in the last five or six years, since I moved to New York, I've had a stronger sense of acceptance than ever before. Sometimes it seems as if I meet new fans—old friends—every day. All the walking I do in New York makes it easier to talk to people, and I love it. In California, everyone's isolated in their separate cars; no one walks anywhere. Rita Moreno said the only way you get to meet someone in Hollywood is if you have a car wreck.

Recently a man introduced himself to me with his wife and showed me a photograph of the two of us together, taken years and years and years ago in Portland during the war. In the yellowing photo, he was a young man; I was a little girl in my Victory Girl uniform. He had saved the picture all this time. He was in tears as he showed it to me; his wife was in tears. And I was in tears. To find out you've touched other lives without even knowing it is wonderful.

I've tried to figure out what it is fans see in me. I sometimes think it's that I'm like everyone's sister, or the daughter they had, or wish they had (everyone's Girl Next Door). It was confusing at first. To me, a star was someone like Betty Grable or Rita Hayworth or Lana Turner, and I didn't play those kinds of parts. I was always wholesome, not sexy. And my fans were wholesome, too, always gentle and kind. No one pushed or shoved or ripped the clothes from my back. They never have. People have always been very polite with me. I was always treated with respect, affection, warmth—like a sister.

It's a funny kind of family, but very special, too. Not always real, like the movies—but filled with memories and a sense of connection.

One of my favorite movie dads (or granddads), Louis Calhern, told me something about memories once, which I was too young to understand. Louie played my grandfather—and Ann Sothern's father—in *Nancy Goes to Rio*, a breezy musical set in South America. I played the usual role, with a risqué plot twist: For a while my innocent young character is mistakenly assumed to be pregnant. During rehearsals Louie loved to reminisce about his days in the theater when he was a matinee idol, and I loved to listen to him. One day, I said to him, "Oh, Louie, you have so many wonderful memories." And he smiled and said, "Just wait, honey, you will too, all too soon."

What did he mean, "too soon"? Well, Louie was right. I do have memories, and they involve him. When I was married to Geary and we held our first dinner party, we invited Louie and his wife, Slats, and Busby Berkeley and his wife to dinner. We had a little apartment on Beverly Glen in Los Angeles. I was so proud of it. I had furnished and decorated it with Duncan Phyfe furniture, our silver wedding gifts, pastoral paintings, and a big television set, which was kept out of sight because no one connected with the studio was allowed to watch TV in those days. And I had a cat, Demitasse—a Siamese cat.

I had been working that day, probably on *Nancy Goes to Rio*, or maybe *A Small Town Girl*. We had a maid, and since it was the first time she had cooked for us, I planned the menu with her. Actually, *she* planned the menu because the only thing she could cook was fried chicken, which I found out later. The four guests arrived, and I was so proud. All the silver was polished, and we were very fancy, I thought. Then we were called to dinner.

The dining room was very small, two steps down from the living room. Because it was so small it was impossible for the maid to serve us, so Geary passed the chicken and the mashed potatoes, gravy, and peas—just like Mama used to make for Sunday dinner. So, when we were all served, I saw Geary talking to the maid. He was asking her, "Do we have any finger bowls?" (Which we didn't.) The maid got a perplexed look on her face and rushed to the kitchen. Within a few minutes she came out with a large silver platter with a big dish on it filled with hot water, and asked, "Does anybody want to wash their hands?" Louie, with all his sophistication, rose to the occasion and said, "I think it's very Chinese," as we passed the plate and the bowl around the table and washed our hands. With that, my cat, Demitasse, who had just fallen into the toilet and was sopping wet, sat on the top step and meowed. I am now about the same age Louie was back then. And now I understand what he said: My memories are ripe, and none too soon.

I wasn't a child when I worked with Louie, though I felt like one. I was about twenty, almost a married woman (but a very *young* twenty). *Nancy Goes to Rio*, which premiered in 1950, was my seventh movie; three others—*Three Daring Daughters, Luxury Liner,* and *A Date with Judy*—had all come out in a burst in 1948. I spent the second half of my teens working almost constantly on one picture or another. I remember the feel of that life more clearly now than any individual movie. My memories—talking earnestly with Louie, sitting beside Elizabeth in a classroom—come in flashes, like half-forgotten scenes from an old film.

Elizabeth Taylor, for instance, is in many of my mental pictures, a beautiful, glowing young girl. She came to MGM a few years after I did and we became friends. We were both doing the same thing, working. I'd go to lessons, she'd go to lessons—we didn't have a real girly-girly kind of relationship—no lunching and gossiping. Later, when Elizabeth became my bridesmaid and I hers, people assumed we were very close, but in fact we just didn't know anyone else to ask. How were we supposed to meet anyone else? We were both working all the time. It was hard to find enough bridesmaids for us. My wedding to Geary came first, Elizabeth's to Nicky Hilton was next. Both weddings were beautiful, but Elizabeth's was a bit more posh. Both were held at the Catholic Church of the Good Shepherd in Beverly Hills—the best game in town.

I don't think any of us felt like stars. We didn't see ourselves as mature, glamorous, special—we were just kids. Elizabeth

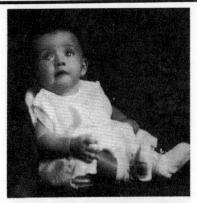

My first portrait.

About age three. Mama made my dress.

Oregon Victory Girl's summer uniform.

War-bond rally when Lana Turner visited Portland.

At world premiere of *Song of the Open Road* in Portland with Mama and Daddy.

Delightfully Dangerous with my good friend Ralph Bellamy, and Arthur Treacher.

Hedda Hopper visiting on the set.

Roddy's first shave.

A Sunday afternoon at Roddy McDowall's. From left: Roddy (back to camera). Virginia McDowall, Jerry Courtland, me, Elizabeth Taylor, Ann Blyth, Darryl Hickman.

My cat, Ginger, made the cover of *Life* magazine. *(Martha Holmes, LIFE magazine, ©1946 Time Inc.)*

Relaxing between rehearsals of the Frank Sinatra radio show with Frank and Irving Berlin.

With one of my favorites, Carmen Miranda.

Laughing, as usual, with George Brent, during the filming of *Luxury Liner*.

With Debbie Reynolds on the set of *Two Weeks with Love.* It was all in fun.

Ricardo Montalban and I fell overboard.

Sissy, Michael Wilding, Jr., his mother, Elizabeth, and I at
G.A.'s birthday party.

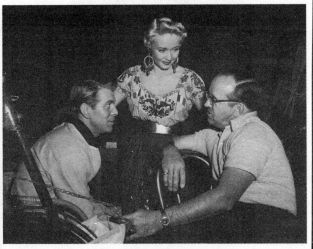

Gene Nelson, Daddy, and I.

Seven Brides for Seven Brothers (©1954 Loews Incorporated. Rev. 1982 Metro-Goldwyn-Mayer Film Co.)

August 24, 1957: G.A. and Sissy, always holding hands.

Talking things over with Fred Astaire on the set of *Royal Wedding*.

The longest song title ever written: "How Could You Believe Me When I Said I Loved You When You Know I've Been A Liar All My Life?" *(© 1951 Loews Incorporated)*

Easter Sunday with the family: Pat, Monie, G.A., Sissy, and Lindsay

Clowning between takes of *Athena* with co-star Vic Damone.

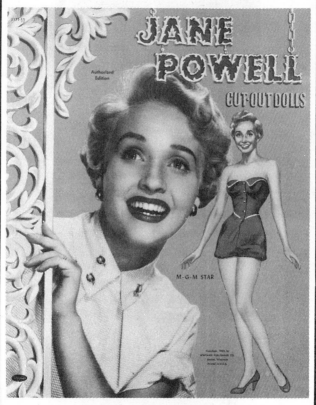

Paper dolls and coloring books are now collector's items.

Irene, my first Broadway show.

The dear, sweet Patsy Kelly. *(Photos: Martha Swope)*

The love of my life.

Sissy, me, and friend.

With Lindsay, my youngest.

The wedding of the year. The groom's mother checks the happy couple, Geary (G.A.) and Maureen.

didn't really like what she was doing, I remember; she couldn't wait to get out. She was shy, too, but her mother liked it, the studio liked it, the public liked it. . . . She was never a gung-ho "star," it just happened to her. Like it happened to me. For her, it came as even more of a surprise—it was mainly her mother's idea, I think. Probably her mother would say it was the other way around; that's what the mothers always say.

We worked together in *A Date with Judy*, in which we both played girls like ourselves. Of course, she was the femme fatale and I was The Girl Next Door. Elizabeth—who was younger than I—got to wear green eyeshadow, show her figure in a tight sweater, and look sexy; that hurt. I was really a little jealous, not of her but of the green eyeshadow.

I'm not usually jealous. And I don't like competition. Even in tennis—I play for the exercise, not to win. Sometimes it amazes me that I got where I am because I have no dog-eat-dog in me. I never felt I was competing with anyone or jealous of anyone. And if I *was* I probably would have denied it. (But just once I would have liked to be the sexy one in a movie.)

In *A Date with Judy* I played Judy, happily involved in a teenage romance with Scotty Beckett until she almost spoils everything by falling for an older man, Robert Stack. Elizabeth played my rich, sexy best friend and rival for Bob's affections. Bob gave me my first screen kiss, but Elizabeth got him in the end. The film was a lightweight musical comedy in which I sang numbers like "It's a Most Unusual Day" and "I'm Strictly on the Corny Side." In *Variety*'s summation: "Talented young Jane Powell registers appealingly with vocals," and Elizabeth Taylor's "breathtaking beauty is complimented by the Technicolor lensing."

Yes, Elizabeth was really beautiful, with breasts and at such an early age. She wore a waist cincher, as most girls did back then, a wide belt you could lace up or hook. I would wear a garter belt to hold up my stockings, or a girdle if I were wearing a straight skirt. It's amazing, considering how small I was, that I had to wear a girdle at all, but in those days no part of a woman was supposed to jiggle.

Anyway, back when I was wearing my girdle, Elizabeth,

with her tiny waist, would come to school in dirndl skirts and lots of petticoats, always fastened with safety pins. Her mother, Sarah, an actress herself, didn't have time for mundane things like needle and thread, so invariably this gorgeous girl would come to school with pins everywhere. Our principal, Miss McDonald, used to keep a box of safety pins just for Elizabeth.

Safety pins and shoes . . . Elizabeth's mom may have been disorganized, but she believed in living the good life. When Elizabeth went shopping, and found a pair of shoes she liked, she would buy them in every color. I would never, *never* buy more than one of anything. I yearned to someday be able to buy those rainbows of shoes. It wasn't a question of money—not anymore—but that was extravagant in my family's book. Elizabeth and her mom treated money like safety pins.

Years later, I went to a bridal shower at Elizabeth's house. I went upstairs to go to the bathroom, and there on her dresser was a mess of tissue paper, Kleenex, hairpins, odds and ends. In the middle of the mess were two pearl rings as big as nickels, one black and one white. I stared for a long time; those beautiful rings, lost in a crumple of soiled Kleenex.

If Louis Calhern was my favorite movie dad, my *least* favorite was Wallace Beery. Beery played my father in *A Date with Judy*. I thought he was a fine actor, and a big cuddly teddy bear—but no. He ignored everybody and everything. He never said hello. He never said good-bye. He never smiled.

When Dick Moore was doing his book on child actors, he asked Margaret O'Brien how they got her to cry in films and she answered, "All they had to do was tell me that Wallace Beery was going to steal the scene." She told Dick they practically had to nail Beery into a box to keep him from maneuvering her out of camera range. I guess this was common knowledge. In a review of *A Date with Judy, Variety* praised Beery for resorting to so "little of his customary mugging." Being forced to perform with so many cute kids must have driven him crazy!

Beery used to steal more than scenes—everything he could get his hands on he would rent back to the studio; and he got away with it. He was stingy. If filming on a picture was coming to an end and he suspected there might be some retakes, he'd take home his entire wardrobe. One time he took a canoe that said PROPERTY OF MGM on the bottom, and rented it to the studio for retakes!

In my first movie of 1948, *Three Daring Daughters*, my character didn't have a dad at first—until her divorced mom, Jeanette MacDonald, managed to snare José Iturbi. Of course, Ann Todd, Mary Eleanor Donahue, and I did everything we could to spoil the romance. This Pasternak production, a comeback vehicle for Jeanette, got awful reviews, although they were kind to me. Bosley Crowther of *The New York Times* called it "a silly little tale" that could be "downright embarrassing in some of the stickier scenes." Jane Powell, he added graciously, was "attractive and melodious." Seymour Peck, writing in the old New York newspaper *P.M.*, said the film provided "115 minutes of almost unmitigated boredom." *Time* magazine added that the whole production seemed "hardly worth the trouble." The complaints were pretty universal, I guess—but I still enjoyed making the film.

Jeanette MacDonald was a very funny lady, but she hadn't done a movie in a long time, and I think she was a bit nervous. She was still the elegant *grande dame* and everyone treated her with deference. Jeanette had a makeup box that she took everywhere; I called it "Pandora's box." Such interesting things came out of it, all kinds of makeup. Again and again she would call for that box and her maid would come rushing over with it. I had to do a crying scene with Jeanette, run into her bedroom, kneel beside her bed, and cry. But every time the tears were flowing just right, she would suddenly stop production and call for her box. So we all had to stop and wait.

When I look back at that little performance, I guess it was quite funny to watch, but at the time I didn't think so. No doubt she thought I'd run out of tears eventually, but there were plenty to go around. Apparently she also used to pull that sort of stunt when she was working with Nelson Eddy. I understand she didn't care for him at all. In any case, she and I got along well; I was very fond of her.

Ann Sothern, my mother in *Nancy Goes to Rio*, was terrific. Actually, we looked a lot alike—we both had round faces. Ann was a real foodaholic. She was always *zaftig*—and loved to eat. She would hide chocolate cakes in her dressing room, underneath her couch, in the closets. She always had a maid with her, and the maid always carried a basket, and in that basket there was always something good to eat. Then Ann would pretend she hadn't eaten anything at all!

My *least* favorite movie mama—and now I'm skipping ahead quite a few years—was Hedy Lamarr. This was in *The Female Animal*, one of the last movies (1958) I ever made and one of the worst. I'd left MGM by then and made the film for Universal. In this movie Hedy Lamarr played my mother, but she didn't like the idea of having a grown-up daughter, even though in real life Hedy did have children. I don't think she'd ever played a mother before, and she was worried about her age; she thought of herself as perennially young. She didn't even want to do any scenes with me, which was a little unreasonable since I was supposed to be her child, and that was the plot of the film.

At the time, I always wore a little diamond necklace. Well, Hedy refused to do the picture until she too could have a little diamond necklace! I thought it was funny, but she got what she asked for. That woman was "star" all the way.

Every morning she would arrive at the studio in her chauffeur-driven limousine and walk directly to the makeup room along a special carpet rolled out before her. And when she arrived, she would immediately lie down flat on her back, and have her face packed in ice. The ice was supposed to reduce bloat and tighten up her skin, but I never thought she needed it.

Once, her children came to watch us work, and one of them said something like "Oh, Mommy, you have so many lines on your face!" That didn't go over very well, and I never saw them on the set again. That same day something the camera-man said made me laugh—something about dressing to the left. Anyway, it had nothing to do with Hedy, but she assumed we were laughing at her. She stalked off the set that evening and didn't come back for three days! What a shame she was so insecure, because she was a real star and an incredibly beautiful woman. But sometimes you can get so wrapped up in beauty you don't think you have anything else. And many times you don't.

Hedy Lamarr was the only actor I ever had problems with. When I was a teenager, all my professional relationships went smoothly; if anyone didn't like me, I didn't know it. Sometimes, even when they *did* like me, I didn't know. I moved through those years at a high speed.

George Brent, for instance: I never realized how much he liked me until later. George was my movie dad in *Luxury Liner*. He played the captain of a luxury cruise ship heading to Rio, and when he refused to let me come along, I stowed away on board. Other passengers included the opera singers Lauritz Melchior and Marina Koshetz, bandleader Xavier Cugat, and Carmen Miranda, so you can imagine the musical and romantic complications. ("Pleasantly diverting froth," commented *Variety*.)

I adored Carmen with her big banana hats and her heart as big as all outdoors. I loved Lauritz Melchior, too. Lauritz never played my father, but he could have. *He* was a big woolly bear—not cold, tall but gentle, jolly, bigger than life, and could he sing! He was a Wagnerian singer with a twinkle in his eye. His dear wife, Kleinchen, was quite a person herself. I love how they met. She literally parachuted into his front yard. She knew how to get her man. The marriage lasted many years, until she died. She was his ears, his eyes, his mentor. What Kleinchen said, went, we knew.

Xavier Cugat carried a little Chihuahua and considered himself quite a ladies' man. He didn't talk much, I remember, but the dog could bark on cue. I wasn't infatuated with Cugat—but I was with George Brent. I was eighteen and he was about forty-five. I had such a crush on him I couldn't stand it. We never even had lunch together, but I thought about him all the time; I couldn't wait until the days when we were both working. He was so good-looking, and fun, and had a wonderful sense of humor. I remember we laughed all the time, though for the life of me, I can't remember why. One time he gave me a skunk. He'd heard I'd always wanted one and found one, but by the time it arrived at the studio it was full-grown and not very friendly. I treasured it anyway—it was from George.

I never saw him after the movie, and I didn't even think of him after a while; schoolgirl crushes have a way of evaporating.

Then a few years ago, when I was doing *South Pacific* with Howard Keel in San Diego, I received a bouquet of long-stemmed roses from him, and a lovely letter. I was so moved. It was the first time I had heard from George since I was eighteen.

In the letter he asked if his daughter, Suzanne (Suzanne— my other name) could come backstage after she saw the show, and of course I said yes. When I met her I told her how much I'd love to see her dad, but she told me he was ill with emphysema and wouldn't go out. He was in his seventies. "He's not too well," I remember she said. I was so disappointed; I really wanted to see him. You know how it is; all of a sudden you can't wait to get in touch with someone from your past, to see if that past can be rekindled. I knew he lived somewhere around San Diego, so I flipped through a telephone directory. Sure enough, he was listed. He answered the phone.

"George, this is Jane," I said. He couldn't put it together for a moment; then his voice got about ten years younger. We talked and talked. I asked him to come to the show, but he said he couldn't.

"Well then, why don't you come up to L.A.?" I said. I was going to be doing *South Pacific* in Los Angeles for the next five weeks.

"I can't," he said. "I don't drive."

"Then why don't you take the train?" I asked.

We talked at least two or three times a week after that conversation, and I knew he was getting more and more anxious to get together; so was I. He made it clear he wanted to see me alone if he did come. Finally, he planned to take the train up, go to the theater, *but* he didn't want to meet me there. "Every time I've seen you," he said, "there have been other people around. That's why I never got to talk to you. You were a little girl—your mother was always around. This time, when I see you I don't want *anyone* else to be around."

He came to a Sunday matinee. I had reserved a house seat for him. Everybody in the cast kept peeking through the curtain to catch a glimpse of him; so did I. He looked like an El Greco painting—thin face, white hair, small goatee. Very slender, straight as a ramrod. Don Quixote. So handsome. He saw the show and left.

The next day, Monday, we were to have dinner. I was so excited. I got all dressed up, thrilled to be going to see him. We met at his suite at the Beverly Wilshire Hotel.

He came to the door, put his finger up to his lips, and said, "Shhh." I thought maybe someone was asleep. But he brought me into the room and led me over to a couch. On the couch was a bathrobe with his monogram and under the robe was a photograph of the two of us, laughing. It was in a broken brown wooden frame. I had autographed the picture for him all those years ago. The glass was broken, too, and he told me he had carried it with him around the world.

Then George told me he had always loved me. He couldn't pursue me when I was a girl, he said—someone was always with me—but he had never forgotten me. We had dinner, and I left feeling warm and excited.

I was tremendously flattered and surprised, but I knew nothing would come of it. I loved him, but I certainly wasn't *in* love with him. I was fascinated, and probably flirtatious; and he was lonely. He lived alone with his small dog, Skipper. How he loved that dog.

We kept talking several times a week. (Now I think maybe I should have broken things off sooner.) I continued the tour of *South Pacific*, and in every new town he sent me flowers, and we talked, long distance. I pushed him to gain weight. I got him vitamins, sent him cards. He seemed so happy, people told me, so suddenly happy. He had a new, mysterious sparkle.

At Christmas I went to visit him. "I have to see you," he said, so I flew down to San Diego. I finally met Skipper, his too fat little dog, and saw his house. It was sparsely decorated, almost bare, with few pictures on the walls, but he had scrapbooks. Although George had said we weren't going to exchange presents, I had brought Skipper a silver bowl.

Then . . . George asked me to marry him. "We could have our own separate lives. You can live in Hollywood, and I can live here," he said. I was shocked. "I can't," I said. "I just can't, George."

I was thinking about marriage, but not to him. When I did get married again, he was furious. He was cold when we talked after that. He got married himself soon after I did, to a woman he'd known in Hawaii for thirty years. But he didn't want to live in Hawaii and she didn't want to live in California. So I presume they lived separate lives, as he said we would have.

George was a sad man, but not because of me. He'd been one of the most loved actors in Hollywood—every woman wanted to work with him and usually fell in love with him—but he seemed bitter. He wasn't very warm toward his children. He was crotchety. "Hello!" he'd bark when I called to check up on him, before he knew who it was.

George died. The day before he passed away, I was going through my telephone book and I saw his name and thought, *I've got to give George a call*. But I didn't. Oh, how I wish I had. He passed away that night. My sweet George. It saddens me so to think I didn't call.

I hope he died a happy man, but I have my doubts.

✳✳ 8 ✳✳

"GOLLY! IMAGINE THIS!" gushes a story in *Movie Stars Parade*. "November fifth was my big day, probably the most important day in my whole life."

The story is signed "Jane Powell," but I didn't write it. My copy is faded now, torn in places, yellow, with that musty smell old newsprint always seems to have. And that's no wonder; it was clipped out almost forty years ago.

"Right now I'm so happy I could burst wide open," exclaims that faded clipping. "And every now and then I have to pinch myself to be sure it's true. But it is true! All of it!"

I had forgotten the day, but on November 5, 1949, I married Geary Anthony Steffen, Jr.

"I'll always remember. A girl has only one wedding," proclaims *Movie Stars Parade*. In fact, I had four. I'm not proud of that; in fact it embarrasses me a lot. "The most important day in my whole life" was just a day after all. I feel sadness, and joy, looking at the yellow clipping. I feel pleasure, too, and deep regret.

I met Geary at Sonja Henie's Ice Skating Palace in West-wood when I was almost eighteen. He was there practicing. Geary was Henie's skating partner and I was so impressed. I'd been bored, looking for something athletic to do, and someone said, Why don't you go ice skating? So I got in my car, excited to be doing something I'd never done, and almost as soon as I got to the rink, I met Geary and he started giving me lessons. It was that simple. I'd been dating other boys—actor Marshall Thompson; Tommy Batten—but once I met Geary he quickly became my one-and-only.

According to a stack of newspapers and fan magazines, my marriage to Geary was something "special." Well, I guess every marriage is special, or should be. What I loved about Geary was his zest for fun. I'd never known anyone like him. I didn't understand this at the time, of course, but I realize now that that is what attracted me. Geary was an athlete, a skater, a skier, a water-skier; he introduced me to that outdoor world I'd always yearned for.

When I was eighteen, Mama and I took a trip to Sun Valley, Idaho. It was my first vacation—and Geary was there. It was a real-life "Sun Valley Serenade." So romantic, just like the movie. Geary himself was romantic. The combination, backed up by the white snow and the sun and hayrides in the moonlight, seemed like a scene in my dream of romance.

Geary and I dated for about two years before we got married, and I was blissfully happy. It's hard to sort it all out now, so *much* of what I felt then was based in fantasy. I had *fun* with Geary, actual, uncomplicated fun. I met a different group of people. I loved the athletic, outdoorsy part of our life. We went skating and to hockey games and to the fights (Geary's father was the fighter Willy Richie), things I hadn't experienced before. All I had ever done athletically was swim—so Geary's world genuinely appealed to me. Genuinely—and falsely.

Geary was not truly gorgeous, but he had a good physique, very slender. Although not handsome, he had a strong face, which showed evidence of skin problems he had when young. I loved to watch him skate. It was a new adventure—for both of us. He hadn't met anyone like me, either.

I thought I loved Geary. Maybe I did. But maybe I just wanted freedom, and a home of my own, and babies.

Our wedding, at the Church of the Good Shepherd in Beverly Hills, was a huge extravaganza. I know almost five hundred invitations were sent out, but I'm not even sure who came. I wanted it to be intimate. I didn't want to invite anyone from the studio, I recall, because I was afraid they'd think I just wanted a present. I'm not even sure if we invited L. B. Mayer! I guess we *must* have, but the truth is, I don't remember. I do remember that Jeanette MacDonald gave me some lovely gold demitasse spoons. I still have them. And I know I got a lot of silver.

I wore white, of course, lace and taffeta, with a fitted bodice, long lace sleeves, and a veil streaming from a little lace bonnet. I carried a bouquet of lilies-of-the-valley and baby white orchids. I helped design the dress myself, with my friend and designer, Helen Rose. Geary wore pearl-gray spats and an ascot. White flowers filled the church, and glowing candles lit my path as I walked slowly down the aisle. Our enormous cake was topped with candy wedding bells.

"Like something out of a fairy story, with me as the princess in a dreamy white gown who was carried away by her knight in gleaming armor," a fan magazine quoted me. But fan mags, like fairy tales, don't tell you what happens after.

Our wedding took place in a Catholic church because Geary was Catholic. However, since I wasn't we couldn't be married in back of the rail. I tried to convert, mostly at the urging of Roddy's mother, who sent me to her priest. I took instructions but there were so many things I just couldn't understand. I wanted to have a religion: Daddy was a Methodist, but lost interest after having to spend all weekend long in church as a child, and Mama didn't care about religion much, so I was always searching for something. I had gone to every church— to the Christian Scientists, to the Catholics, the Presbyterians, even to synagogue—but I hadn't found the answers. I really tried to believe, but soon realized I couldn't join the club!

Our children were baptized Catholic, since the Church insisted on it, but I was never baptized myself until years later when I became an Episcopalian.

Back when I was twenty, Geary was the only husband I could imagine having. In addition to Elizabeth, my other bridesmaids included Roddy's sister, Virginia, Betty Sullivan

(Ed Sullivan's daughter), and my good friend and stand-in Margie Dillon. Geary's sister, Barbara Covington, acted as matron of honor (wearing, my fan mag reports, "an off-the-shoulder lavender taffeta gown with a fitted bodice") and Roddy, of course, was an usher and my moral support. After the ceremony we hosted a lavish reception in the Crystal Room at the Beverly Hills Hotel.

There were presents of all descriptions from friends, family, and fans. It was overwhelming—silver egg cups, platters, perfume bottles, dishes, candlesticks—and some things I never did figure out.

When the dust had settled and Geary and I were back from our honeymoon, I started to take inventory. What a dilemma. Circa 1780, circa 1850, circa this, circa that—what did they all mean? I received so much silver, I felt I had to exchange some. I called Allen Adler, the silversmith from whom most of the gifts came, and explained my predicament. Oh, I was so naïve. "Mr. Adler," I said, "maybe you can help me. I have so many 'circas' here, I wonder if I could exchange some for something else." I'm sure he was rolling on the floor at hearing this woman-child who wanted to exchange circas for something else. No one ever told me that circa meant "around"—none of my folks knew a circa from a circus.

So much about that wedding seems poignant now, sadly ironic. The press treated it almost like a royal coronation. I wanted family closeness, but instead of being happy for me, my mother was hurt that I would leave her, I guess. I still don't understand for certain why Mama turned away from me when I got married. It's been almost forty years—and several more marriages for both of us—and I'm still not sure why.

I warned Mama when I was seventeen that she should find another interest in life, another interest besides me, and she agreed. But she never did. Then suddenly she wasn't there. She could have shared my new life, been a grandmother to my children. Instead, she walked away. But it was time for me to get married and have a house and babies.

Mama said, "Now that you're a married woman, you don't have time for me anymore." *I* didn't have time for *her*! She walked away from Daddy, too. But now Daddy and I had more time together.

More irony: "My Geary has a fine family," I supposedly wrote in *Movie Stars Parade*. "His mother and father have always been wonderful to me. Best of all they have treated me just like a daughter. It always makes me feel warm inside." But in fact, I found out much later, Geary's mother thought I was the most unattractive girl she knew. "How could he marry that ugly girl?" she said. I guess she wasn't any happier about our wedding than Mama was. I also liked Geary's sister, Barbara, who lived in a cozy, picture-postcard California town. I loved to go skiing there—it was folksy and wonderful.

I always thought Geary's mom cared about me, even loved me, but our divorce three and a half years later taught me a lot. She was a very pretty woman, I remember, tall with graying hair; she looked like a picture of someone's attractive mother. We would laugh and talk together—I felt that I could tell her about all sorts of things, intimate things I couldn't talk about to Mama.

But when she wrote me a terrible letter when we were getting divorced I found out differently. Another mother had divorced me.

More irony: My fan magazine is full of talk of forever, of this one special never-to-be-repeated day in a girl's lifetime, of my dreams of a big family, a house full of children. "Geary and I are planning a wonderful family," I said. "We hope for a boy and girl right at first. And after that . . . I'd like ten in all." My sadness in reading these naïve lines, even though I didn't actually write them, is especially sharp. Because this time the old wedding report isn't wrong: I really *did* have those dreams, and I believed them. We had our boy and our girl. But it just wasn't enough.

We were happy at first; it was like playing house. It was all so new to me. I'd never been away from home, I'd never lived with anyone but my parents. Now I had to get used to this almost-stranger.

I honestly thought I would get pregnant the first time I had sex. After marrying Geary, I wanted to have children right away and was amazed when we didn't. I actually went to a doctor, I was so afraid something was wrong with me. The doctor explained it to me a little, but not enough.

The press, of course, was thrilled by our marriage—much more so than our own families. The Girl Next Door was *supposed* to get married, was supposed to pick an athletic, all-American boy. Once again I'd pleased my public by living out their fantasies, and mine.

You can imagine, or maybe you can't, all the pictures of me and Geary—of our house, the dogs, the cats, the car, the swimming pool, and then, of course, the babies. Pictures of me pregnant ("Janie went right into her junior size seven dresses after little Geary was born, plans to do the same after number two debuts"); of diapers on the line; of Jane and darling tots in Disneyland. I wasn't the first Hollywood Girl Next Door, but I don't remember seeing photos of Deanna Durbin cooking in the kitchen. I was in those kinds of pictures all the time.

The fan magazines would plan baby showers or dinners or picnics in the park or swimming-pool parties, and they would invite people and bring all the food and set the tables. Do everything. The event might be at Geary's and my house, or it might be anywhere else the magazine wanted it. And I'd come and pose in their chosen setting and pretend to be eating—or even cooking! Even though I loved to cook on these planned occasions, the magazine did everything but smile for the camera.

We did entertain a lot, and I did a lot of cooking. Our house was always filled with people. It was always time for play. It seemed Geary was happier being with his friends than with me. I guess I didn't feel it at first, with all the romance and excitement of being married, but after a year or so I started wondering. I started asking myself questions I wasn't supposed to ask.

If only I'd had girlfriends to talk to, I might have started asking questions sooner. At least I might have trusted my judgment, trusted my sense that something was wrong. (Possibly I wouldn't have married Geary at all.) I felt Geary didn't love me. He treated everyone the same—the dog, the maid, the paper boy, friends, enemies, it didn't matter. I wasn't special, and neither were the children. He loved the whole world and no one in particular. But I thought I *should* be special to my husband. Geary told me I was wrong. He said, "You are *supposed* to love everyone the same."

"It's impossible to love everyone the same," I said. But I wasn't sure; I didn't know how to trust my judgment. He said I was wrong. "It's hypocritical," I said. But he told me again I was wrong. This didn't make sense to me. It took me a while to figure things out, but our relationship probably lasted longer than it would have had I trusted myself earlier.

I made three movies, including two of my favorites, during the first two years of my marriage to Geary. My personal favorite is the one I plunged into right after our wedding—*Two Weeks with Love* with Louis Calhern, Debbie Reynolds, and my good friend Ricardo Montalban.

I loved making *Two Weeks with Love* because it was a very special experience. The cast was so wonderful, I feel happy even now when I think about the film. "I get a glow," I once told Hedda Hopper.

Hedda Hopper was very good to me. She was one of the most important gossip columnists in Hollywood. We had known each other from my beginnings in Hollywood when I was on her radio show.

I visited her one Christmas at home, and we were talking about buying business gifts. She said, "Come with me, Janie." She led me up the stairs and opened a room at the end of the hall. There, stacked from floor to ceiling were gifts in every shape and size, many of them still wrapped. "Janie," she said, "these are gifts of fear."

I was twenty-one when *Two Weeks with Love* premiered. In it I played a naïve seventeen-year-old who's dying to turn eighteen and wear a corset. The movie was set in the early 1900s, when a corset was supposed to be the height of female charm. It was my first period picture, and I loved it. I think I was born in the wrong century. Ann Harding played my mother, Louis Calhern was my dad, and Debbie Reynolds played my younger sister. (Much later on, I replaced Debbie in the Broadway hit *Irene*.)

I remember that Louie said it was ridiculous playing the father of Debbie and me. "It's the grossest bit of miscasting I ever saw," he said. "Me, with my long nose, and being as tall as I am, playing the father of two little button noses like Janie and Debbie!"

My favorite part of *Two Weeks with Love* was a dream sequence when I got to dress like a femme fatale and sing "My Hero" to Ricardo Montalban. It was a wonderful sequence, a young girl's fantasy. I wore a pink satin corset with long black silk stockings, long white kid gloves, shoes with rhinestone buckles, and a big pink-tulle picture hat. I twirled a pink ruffled umbrella and had a painted beauty mark on my face. Ricardo lifted me in the air, and we waltzed. What a fantasy!

I'd known Ricardo and his wife, Georgiana, for years, long before I was married. We were friends, but when Ricardo was playing my sweetheart, I did develop quite a crush on him. It was just a crush, nothing more, believe me.

I could never call Ricardo "Rick." Some people did, but it just seemed wrong to me; it still does. He is Ricardo and always will be. He has a great Latin flair and an excitable Latin disposition, too. He is very manly, very strong, very deep. I love spending time with him, he is so interesting and interested; he seems curious about everything and I admire that. He is kind, volatile. . . . Listen to me! You can see I still remember that crush.

I would never have *dreamed* of having an affair with Ricardo or anyone. I probably did flirt. I'd never flirted before—or if I did, I didn't know it. Now, all of a sudden, I did it and I knew it. Somehow I had changed.

Maybe now that I was married I felt more like a woman than I had before. And maybe I knew there was something wrong at home. There was no affair, but in my mind the flirtation was an affair, and I felt guilty.

One time, when I was on the road doing the theater circuit, I became infatuated with a comic who was on the bill with me.

He was funny and easy to be with; and he was clearly attracted to me. G.A. had just been born.

These romances were both thrilling and shameful to me.

I didn't want to admit to the idea that I would even look at another. I believed that when a woman got married she was never supposed to be aware of anyone but her husband. So I felt terribly guilty, but I don't think Geary suspected anything. I don't think he noticed me enough to detect a change in me. Maybe if he had known, he wouldn't have cared.

In a way, I think Geary wasn't mature enough to be a good husband. Or perhaps he just couldn't be a good husband to *me*. Or maybe I couldn't be a good wife to him. I just know something about that marriage sent me looking elsewhere for escape. I was eager to have children—maybe that would help. But nothing helped.

I got married for the wrong reasons, and I married the wrong man. A lot of naïve young women hurried to get married in those days; women, girls really, eager to be grown up, eager to be accepted, to get away from home, have sex! Eager for that kind of success, the success of "catching a man" and settling down. It was time!

I felt all of that. I had a role—I wanted to play it well. I had a sense of obligation; if my fans wanted a glorious wedding, I'd give it to them. If The Girl Next Door was supposed to be married and have babies, then how could I do anything else? I was a professional, I was reliable, and everyone was watching.

Everyone was always watching—even I watched. It wasn't just my fans who wanted The Girl Next Door to have a storybook life.

It was me, too.

** 9 **

I STILL THINK of 1951 as a year of milestones. In March, a month before my twenty-second birthday, *Royal Wedding* premiered. We had made it the year before, and it was the first film in which I played an adult. I got the role quite by accident—I replaced *both* June Allyson and Judy Garland! June was taken pregnant and Judy was taken ill. Then, on July 21, I gave birth to my first child, our son, G.A. (pronounced Jay), named Geary Anthony Steffen III after his dad.

I was so thrilled when G.A. finally came along! I'd always said I wanted ten children. Ten was a ridiculous number, I know; I think I just picked it because it sounded round and impressive. But I did love the idea of a big house full of children. I wanted the sort of family you read about in books like *Little Women*.

Despite (or maybe because of) my eagerness to be pregnant, it took Geary and me almost a year to conceive. When it finally happened I was ecstatic. I loved *being* pregnant, the whole process, even though I was sick as a dog for three or four months. I was pregnant twice during the three and a half years I was married to Geary—our daughter, Suzanne Ilene (know as Sissy), was born on November 21, 1952—and both times I was sick, and both times I was blissfully happy. I felt clean, productive, virtuous, radiant as an Ivory soap commercial: For the first time I really felt like a woman.

I'd just about completed work on *Royal Wedding* when I found out I was pregnant with G.A. *Royal Wedding* was my first important film, if you call Hollywood musicals important. At that time musicals were thought of as froth and fun—nothing else. In this movie Fred Astaire and I played brother and sister. (His real sister and dance partner, Adele, never appeared in movies.)

Royal Wedding was produced by Arthur Freed (not Joe Pasternak) and directed by Stanley Donen. Astaire and I, a Broadway dance team, were opening a show in London amid mad preparations for the upcoming marriage of Prince Philip and Crown Princess Elizabeth. It was a runaway hit. Our big number had the world's longest title, "How Could You Believe Me When I Said I Loved You When You Know I've Been a Liar All My Life." I also got to sing a beautiful love song, "Too Late Now," to Peter Lawford, an English lord who made my heart thump (and Fred got to moon over Sarah Churchill, the real-life daughter of Britain's former prime minister). Needless to say, we all ended up getting married on the same day as the royal couple.

Our reviews were excellent. (I'd never taken dancing seriously and we certainly didn't have much time for rehearsal. Fred and I didn't rehearse together much because he had already taught June and Judy the dance routines!) *Variety*'s comment was typical: "As a dance partner Miss Powell serves very well; her pert cuteness making up anything lacking in interpreting ability." (The *Times* praised "Fred Astaire beating his tootsies and Jane Powell beating her gums," which was probably a pretty fair appraisal.)

I'd never met Fred until *Royal Wedding*, and I never got to know him very well. But I found him to be gentle, very sweet, and very private. He was quiet and retiring. In person he didn't have the vitality that you would expect from watching him perform. Years later, when I was doing *Irene* on Broadway, the BBC was interviewing Astaire's former dance partners. I said, "I'm afraid I have nothing to tell you because I never knew him." And the interviewer said, "Neither did anyone else. Everyone felt that way."

I thought he didn't like me. I thought he felt that I was too young and that I wasn't a good enough dancer. I thought he would rather have someone else, someone like Cyd Charisse.

I'll never forget the first time Fred and I met. As usual, I was awestruck and didn't know what to say to him. I hesitated and then said, "Mr. Astaire, I understand that you and your sister used to dance together." (Actually, *Royal Wedding* was based somewhat on their life.)

He said, "Yes, we did."

And then I asked, "When did you stop dancing with her?"

"Oh"—he thought for a moment—"about 1929, I think."

And I replied, "Oh, that's the year I was born!"

There was a pause. "They just keep getting younger every year," he muttered, smiled, and walked away.

Fred's first wife was on the set a great deal of the time. I don't know if that was for his protection or for hers. He was anything but snooty, but she seemed to have an air about her. She was always "Mrs. Astaire." A chair would be brought for her and she would sit and watch, but never smile. I think she said hello to me once. Astaire was always very boyish with her, almost nervous, which fascinated me, since he was so authoritative otherwise.

I had to learn all the numbers in three weeks, which at the time was quite a feat. I rehearsed privately because the numbers had already been set, so I didn't get to spend much time alone with him. It took quite a while to shoot the movie, because they'd film one of the dance sequences and then do part of the book; and then go into rehearsal and start working on another dance sequence, but that was usual. We never got to London. Actually we were back on the old back lot.

Fred didn't really dance on his hotel-room ceiling, either. His "human fly" number was filmed in a rotating drum. The room with all its furniture, lamps, and pictures was built inside the drum, with the furniture and the camera carefully secured in place. Fred just danced in the usual upright position while the drum turned slowly. It was a showstopper.

I was supposed to be in love with Peter Lawford in the film, but he was much too cool for me in person. He had a snappy kind of arrogance I didn't appreciate. "Astorpeerious." I coined that word years ago when Daddy would say, "She acts like Astor's pet horse." Peter wasn't interested in me at all. He was a surfer, and I wasn't enough of a glamour girl. One image of him sticks with me: In the film Peter walks out of the church wearing a top hat and tails, but in reality he has nothing on his feet. He was a confident, handsome, formally attired man with dirty bare feet.

Sarah Churchill was said to have studied ballet, but she was not a good dancer. I had never heard of Sarah Churchill, and when her name was mentioned, I asked, "Who?" "Winston Churchill's daughter. She's a great dancer," the powers said, until they saw her dance.

Fred is certainly missed. He was unique. He left us all so much. I hope he knows how much the world loved him.

During both pregnancies I kept working as much as I could. Although I was almost through with *Royal Wedding* by the time I found out I was pregnant, work on *Rich, Young and Pretty*—which premiered in July 1951, the same month G.A. was born—was just beginning. And when I was pregnant with Sissy I was busy filming *Small Town Girl*. I was so sick during that picture I can hardly remember a thing about it, just Bobby Van's miraculous dance number, "Take Me to Broadway," in which he hopped as though he were on a pogo stick throughout the whole number.

I do remember—vividly—working on *Rich, Young and Pretty* and trying desperately not to throw up. I was a lovely shade of green most of the time. The studio sent a car for me every day because I couldn't drive; I could barely stand up.

In *Rich, Young and Pretty* I played a cheery, bouncy Texas girl who visits Paris and finds romance (with Vic Damone) and a long-lost mother (Danielle Darrieux). ("Pretty as a picture postcard," commented *The New York Times*, "and just about as exciting.") I didn't feel so bouncy. I introduced "Wonder Why," a nice song, and had duets with Vic. We sang one dumb song called "How Do You Like Your Eggs in the Morning." That *really* turned my stomach, for more reasons than one.

I'd hoped—now that I was about to become a mother, and now that *Royal Wedding* was such a hit—that the studio would start offering me more mature roles. Instead, I was playing yet another teenage charmer, another bobby-soxer with a permanent toothpaste smile. (The *Times* called me "fetching and cheerful." Wouldn't you know?)

Rich, Young and Pretty was Vic Damone's first film, but I had met him a few years earlier when I was at the Capitol Theater in New York. Joey Adams, who was a stand-up comic back then, told me there was a young man, a singer, who was dying to meet me. They brought Vic backstage, and Joey asked Mama if it would be all right if he took Vic and me to the Copacabana for supper and dancing. After agonizing minutes of deliberation, Mama finally agreed. I remember dancing with Vic while he sang in my ear, all night, and loud.

The next day he sent me a gold necklace with little rubies in it. I was surprised (and delighted). I accepted it, but Mama made me send it back. She said it wasn't proper, getting a gift from a man I hardly knew. She was right, but I really wanted the necklace. Fortunately, Vic refused to take it back. I kept it for years, but it was stolen along with many other good memories. I didn't see Vic again until we did *Rich, Young and Pretty* together. I doubt if I was what he had expected, my being green most of the time!

It was Joe Pasternak who discovered Vic. Pasternak had always been interested in singers, and Vic had, and still does have, the most glorious voice. He had his nose fixed after we did the picture. Now that he was going to be part of Pasternak's stable, I guess he thought it was important—or perhaps the studio thought it was important—that he look more like Hollywood's idea of a leading man.

I played *another* sweet, bubbleheaded young thing in *Small Town Girl*, a musical remake of a 1936 Janet Gaynor film. This time Farley Granger was my love interest, Robert Keith and Fay Wray played my parents, and Ann Miller portrayed a tap-dancing fortune hunter who had her eye on my rich sweetie, Farley. (She didn't get him.) My dad, a small-town judge, put Farley in jail for speeding, and I sang my way into his heart.

After that film, Ann Miller and I became good friends; we still are. (We call each other Mutt and Jeff. Guess who's Mutt?) One time, we traveled together to Rio for a Brazilian film festival, and that's when we really became close. Jeanette MacDonald went along, too, as well as Gene Raymond, Irene Dunne and her husband, and Bob Cummings and his wife, Mary. We all posed outside the plane before it took off. Everyone but Jeanette; she was superstitious about posing for pictures in front of a plane. She also carried her own bottled water and her own pillows with her; why not?

Our plane was a sleeper—this was back in the days when there were such things. I woke up the first morning out of L.A. and saw everyone scurrying around looking for something. But no one seemed quite sure what they were looking for. "Something of Ann's," people said. "Ann has lost something." I went to the bathroom in the back of the plane and there she was, sitting on the closed toilet seat, with her arms flung over her chest.

"Annie, what's wrong?" I asked.

"I lost Moe and Joe," she said. "Moe and Joe."

"Who are Moe and Joe?" I asked.

"My flop chickies," she answered tearfully. She had lost her bust pads. Annie has such endearing names for everything. "Moe" and "Joe" were finally found, having accidentally been made up in her bunk. Soon all was well on Annie's front.

Annie would be the first to tell you that she's just no good at practical things—and doesn't want to learn. She's the one person I know who literally can't boil water, and she keeps it that way. On her passport, where it says "Profession," one time, she wrote in *"star."* She is unique.

Later we were in two more films together, *Deep in My Heart* and *Hit the Deck*, my last MGM movie.

Despite all the queasiness, I recall my pregnancies—all three of them—as glowing, upbeat times. My third child, a daughter, Lindsay, was born in 1956, when I was married to Pat

Nerney. There's something so marvelously *hopeful* about pregnancy, about starting a new unspoiled life. It's later, when a child gets on the wrong path that despair sets in, when you feel as if you don't know your children and wonder where you went wrong. We all want the best for our children.

To a twenty-one-year-old, pregnant for the first time, children meant only sunny times, coloring books, stuffed panda bears, family pictures . . . those were my images of motherhood. I even ironed G.A.'s baby socks. I thought that would make me a good mother.

Of course, all the fan magazines took pictures of me pregnant, of my baby showers, of me buying maternity clothes, of me and the babies. ("There's a new look on Jane Powell's face these days," said one fan mag. "Her expressive features [have] lost their childlike quality, and in its place a womanliness shines through." How flowery.) Speaking of photographers, I remember one shower given for me very clearly. It was a big bash given by my friend actress Betty Lynn. She invited Janet Leigh and Tony Curtis (this was before they were married), and Betty said Janet asked her, "Will there be any photographers there?"

And she answered, "No, we don't want it to be a publicity shower. It's just for fun."

Janet said, "I'm sorry, but we have somewhere else to go, business, you know." Many actors felt an obligation to stay in the public eye.

When I was pregnant with G.A. and Sissy, I designed all my maternity clothes. I had read about the Empress Josephine, Napoleon's wife, who created the Empire dress style when she was pregnant, and my designs were based on that style. We were very social in those days, and I needed clothes I could wear to dinner parties and premieres. Pregnancy didn't slow me down much. Even when I felt sick, I somehow managed to show up at one event or another to show off my big stomach.

Designing my own maternity wardrobe didn't seem unusual to me. I had to have all my clothes made anyway because I was so small. There was no such thing as junior clothes in those days. For years I'd had everything made—hats, gowns, petticoats, even underwear.

When I look back now on motherhood, after some thirty years, I see an uncertain young woman, just out of girlhood, younger than her years, trying to cope with the needy, demanding, dependent new lives she had created, and feeling everything would be just like a movie, happy and fun. I think if I had known then what I know now I would have been *terrified*, or I should have been.

We named G.A. after Geary. I've never liked "juniors" much. It seems egotistical somehow, so he was G.A. I did name Sissy "Suzanne." I'd always liked the name, and since I wasn't using it, I never felt that Sissy was named after me. Her middle name, Ilene, sounds the same as Mama's, but Mama spells hers Eileen.

We started calling Sissy by her nickname right away—from her initials, S.I.S.: Suzanne Ilene Steffen.

I loved having children, just being with them, dressing them up, taking them places, talking to them, showing them off like pretty little dolls. But I never cared to play with them, probably because I didn't know how. When they were babies I told them, "I love being with you, I love having you with me, I love you, but don't ask me to play games." But when I did, they would get so excited.

In a way I'd been "playing" all my life, so maybe it's not surprising that when it came time for me to play with my children, I was simply incapable of it; or *maybe* I was just like Mama.

When they were little, we always seemed to be appearing in publicity photos—birthday parties, Easter parades, excursions to the zoo, that sort of thing. There are pictures of G.A. and Elizabeth Taylor's son, Michael, at their joint birthday party, and of Sissy, at eighteen months, in a little ruffled dress and lace bonnet attending the party of James Mason's five-year-old daughter, Portland. In another, I'm holding G.A. in one arm and Sissy in the other. The caption reads: HAPPY TWOSOME, but we all look fairly uncomfortable. In a photo spread titled BABES IN TOYLAND, I'm shown leading two-year-old G.A. through an emporium called Uncle Bernie's Toy Menagerie. (I pose in a red fire fighter's hat, G.A. atop a fluffy white dog.)

I'm sure being a first-time mother is hard for anyone. It was doubly hard for me—for anyone the press is interested in—because everyone was watching.

G.A. was an adorable little boy, but there was a sadness in his eyes. You can see it when you look at pictures of him as a child. Even the painting Paul Clemens did of him when he was nine has that same haunting sadness. He was always a sensitive child, a beautiful, frail, sad boy, often crying.

As a child G.A. was also short—he's not now—and that always bothered him. He was the shortest boy in his class. Of course, he wanted to be macho, like his father; he wanted to be athletic and strong, like Geary. He would try to compete with Geary, but rarely won. And he tried *so* hard! Geary never had much sympathy for the children, for their feelings. He would be interested in what they were playing, but would never sit down and listen or discuss things, or just talk to them. And if they tried to explain something that had upset them, he'd say, "Oh, that's ridiculous." He didn't know how to give compassion, just as I didn't know how to play.

G.A. was always competitive with his father—Geary was competitive, too, just like another child. Later, after we were divorced, when Geary would bring him home after a visit, G.A. would be nervous. He loved his father, but after they had spent a few hours together he'd be trembling from frustration. He was torn apart. It was hard to watch, but I couldn't stop him from visiting his father. G.A. *wanted* to see him.

When G.A. was a little older, he became more concerned about his height. At least once a month I'd sit down on the edge of his bed and talk about it with him. "They call me shrimp at school," he would say. "They laugh at me." "They didn't pick me for the team."

"Kids are so mean to each other," I would tell him. "Everyone goes through this, sweetheart. Look at Lindsay; they call her 'Four Eyes' because of her glasses. Some people have freckles, some people are skinny, some people are fat, some people are tall. So they're called 'Skinny,' or 'Freckles,' or whatever. They called me 'Stuck-up.' " These talks helped for a time, but the effect wouldn't last. And his father would just laugh and change the subject.

G.A. and Sissy were always together when they were small. She didn't start talking until she was three because he interpreted for her. She would point and grunt. "What does she want?" I would ask, and he would tell me. Sissy didn't walk at an early age, either, but she certainly could crawl fast (the fastest "crawl" in the West!). She was darling, a Campbell's Soup baby, with a Buster Brown haircut and a little round face, bright red cheeks, and clear blue eyes. She looked like a little Kewpie doll.

Sissy was always a quiet child, and aloof, and G.A. was very protective of her. They were only sixteen months apart, but it was clear he knew he was her *big* brother and took the responsibility very seriously. In every picture I have of that time, he's holding her hand.

I wish they felt that way today. None of my children are close. G.A. and Sissy are like strangers. The children grew and changed, and I grew and changed. But sometimes, in some ways, I wish we hadn't.

✱✱ *10* ✱✱

HOLLYWOOD'S DREAM COUPLE, with Dream Babies and Dream House. The dream Hollywood was sure would never die, died.

I killed it.

"This girl is getting married only *once*, and that one time will be just right," I confidently told a fan magazine. But I was wrong.

Jane and Geary "are terrific together," said the fan magazines. Jane and Geary are "the perfect picture of the Ideal Young American Family." "Jane is Movietown's prize example of the model young wife and mother."

What did they know?

In November 1952, Sissy was born. A few months later, in February, MGM loaned me out to Warner Brothers to star with Gordon MacRae and Gene Nelson in *Three Sailors and a Girl*. By April, I was telling Geary that I wasn't happy with him. On August 6, 1953, I filed for divorce. I had fallen for Gene Nelson.

By November, when *Three Sailors and a Girl* opened, Geary and I were squabbling over money, custody, and everything else.

All during the fall of 1953, the movie magazines featured smiling pictures of me and Gene. Not that the magazines *approved* of our attachment. Not at all, but this was news.

"Could Divorce Wreck Jane Powell's Career?" they asked.

"Is Jane Powell Heartless?" they asked.

"What Price Love?" they asked.

Another journalist quoted me—"I tried to kill my love for Gene"—then added. "But you didn't try hard enough, did you, Jane?"

One magazine featured photos of Gene and me, under the headline HEEDLESS HEARTS, and commented, "Three small children feel the deepest hurt." (Lindsay wasn't born yet; the third hurt child was Gene's six-year-old son, Chris.)

And *Movie Magazine* summed it all up: "Another black eye for Hollywood, another decent young girl gone haywire."

If you've ever gone through a divorce, or ever worried that a choice you made might hurt your children, you can imagine how I felt, having every move, every most private decision scrutinized by *the world*.

But all the while I heard Mama's words in my ears. "We only stayed together because of you, honey." What a burden to put on someone—especially a child. I was afraid I might say those same words to my children.

I thought about leaving my husband, and the magazines wrote about "earthquakes." I was seen dancing with Gene, and the magazines wrote about "shock." I filed for divorce, and the magazines wrote about "betrayal."

I had kept so busy during those years that it took me a while to notice that things weren't right at home. I kept on performing after the children were born. It was necessary financially. I made five movies between our marriage in 1949 and our divorce in 1953. In fact, when G.A. was an infant—only seven weeks old—and I was on hiatus I took him on the road with me on one of my vaudeville tours. We went to New York, Buffalo, Cleveland, and Chicago. Geary didn't come with me, just a baby nurse and G.A. (plus all his bottles and goat's milk, which was all he could drink). When we arrived in Chicago, goat's milk was nowhere to be found. I have vague memories of the nurse, the bellman, and I searching everywhere in panic and finally finding canned goat's milk in an out-of-the-way mom-and-pop store somewhere.

Once, we took a late-night train from Buffalo to Cleveland. I rushed to the train with the nurse, the baby, the bottles, the costumes, and arrived in Cleveland at four-thirty in the morning. We were the only people who got off. In those days there were porters and one of them took my bags, which were filled with costumes—and heavy.

There I was with the nurse, the baby, the bottles, the suitcases, and the costumes. The porter politely asked, "Ma'am, do all you actresses carry your own scenery?" Tired as I was, it made me laugh. We were a sight.

The taxi took us to a hotel—and was that a hotel! We had the "bridal suite," which was done in red flocked wallpaper, a red couch, and very subdued lighting. The lampshades were covered with red tassels. It didn't take much imagination to figure out what had gone on in the room the night before! I suspect it looked like a Chinese whorehouse, though I've never seen one. Everything was old and dirty, covered with dust and encrusted grime.

It was still very early in the morning, and I had to be at the theater by eight-thirty to rehearse with the orchestra. We had to do our first show at ten-thirty. I was exhausted, but couldn't sleep. I wouldn't put G.A. down, the place was so filthy. I just held him in my arms and cried.

We moved into the Statler Hotel that morning before showtime. It was *clean*, with cheerful "This Has Been Sanitized" paper strips on the toilet seats! I felt safe. We even managed to find canned goat's milk for G.A. He fared very well, the nurse fared very well—and I collapsed with exhaustion at my last performance and finally was able to go home.

I had gone back to work shortly after G.A. was born, rehearsing dance routines with Nick Castle for my tour. I'd always liked working with Nick. He choreographed *Royal Wedding* and several of my other movies. He was terrific. Fred Astaire normally worked with Hermes Pan—Fred and Hermes walked alike, talked alike, even looked alike, so Nick's job wasn't easy.

Nick had a naughty mouth, and a heart of gold. He would sing wonderful off-color lyrics everyone loved. How he made me laugh, and he had the dirtiest mind of anyone I knew, but I loved it—and him. It was Nick who had gently pointed out to me that girls were supposed to shave their legs and under their arms.

With G.A. and Sissy only sixteen months apart, there wasn't much time to do anything but take care of them and work. I had a wonderful nurse-housekeeper, Gladys—the same nurse who went on the road with me and G.A.—and she really held things together. She did everything. G.A. called her "Dadoo" because he couldn't say Gladys. I know I couldn't possibly have kept working without help, but sometimes I was a little jealous of Gladys's attachment to my babies.

I worried a lot about whether I was a good mother. If you've never been one, how do you know what to do? Several books on parenting had come out, but I didn't read them. Everyone I knew was reading them, and being permissive, letting their children run wild. And I didn't agree with that. Still, I worried.

I remember telling G.A. when he was older: "If I ever did anything to hurt you, in any way, it was not on purpose. It was out of ignorance on my part. I'd never *been* a mother before."

I had two babies in three and a half years, made movies, went on the road, and never seemed to get tired. Or if I did, as my doctor told me recently, I didn't know it. "You don't realize when you're tired," he said. I used to be so wound up, I could never sit still. I would be drinking tea, knitting, talking, watching TV, all at the same time. I always had to keep my hands busy.

I realize now that my energy helped me avoid facing my problems. I was always running, probably running away.

I knew *something* was wrong with our marriage, but I thought it was *me*. It's hard enough dissolving any marriage, admitting you made a mistake, tearing apart bonds that were supposed to last forever; it's even harder when the world is still dancing at your wedding.

Part of Geary's and my difficulty was our different attitudes. He was more interested in having a good time than in earning a living. He liked tennis, skiing, being surrounded by crowds of friends. I liked spending a quiet evening at home with just us. After we'd been married for a while, it seemed he was playing more and more and the house was filled with more people.

When we got married he borrowed five hundred dollars to go into the insurance business. The next year he paid it back. The year after that, he made one thousand dollars and then we divorced, and I paid him half of everything I had for several years. So the divorce was very profitable for him—in effect, for that period, I was paying him alimony. He was supposed to pay for child support, but I rarely received it. I know this is very common; men often walk away from their responsibilities when a marriage fails.

Later, after Geary and I were separated, he took all the Christmas ornaments—the ones I had saved and collected for years and was keeping for the children. Geary had bought a restaurant and wanted to decorate the restaurant tree. Funny how the little things hurt. I was outraged that he would do that to the children.

Geary was a "time to play" father. I guess he was a "time to play" husband, too. I was *trying* to grow up—maybe he was trying hard *not* to.

When MGM loaned me out to Warner's the thought of leaving Geary never entered my mind, at least not consciously. I'd known Gene Nelson slightly before *Three Sailors and a Girl*—I thought he was a terrific dancer—but I certainly didn't think of him as a potential romantic partner. Not only was *I* married; Gene and his wife, Miriam, had been together for more than eleven years.

It seemed impossible.

In *Three Sailors and a Girl* my on-screen romance in this fizzy Sammy Cahn entertainment was with Gordon MacRae— but my off-screen romance with Gene was all anyone really cared about.

I was quite fond of Gordon; he had a wonderful boyish quality that he kept all his life. I don't think he much liked working—he preferred playing golf.

Several years ago we performed in some nightclubs together. By then Gordon had joined Alcoholics Anonymous and was working hard to help others. He still had his boyish quality, but the golf game had gone. As always, he was charming, but quieter than before, as if he'd been through some difficult times. Gordon died a few years ago, and I miss him.

But I only had eyes for Gene. He was sweet, and at first it was just nice to have someone to *talk* to. That's what started it all—talking. Then one thing led to another.

I fell head over heels in love. The four of us—Gene, Miriam, Geary, and I—had problems, but no one walks away if *he* isn't ready to walk and vice versa: No one walks into a perfect situation and changes things. In a way, the timing was right; Gene and I met when we were both unhappy. But our love was real; or I thought it was.

In my mind you didn't have affairs. If you fell in love, you got married; if you had an affair, you got a divorce. The rules were very simple—and I broke them all.

I might as well have been Ingrid Bergman when she had her son out of wedlock—I don't think the public reaction would have been any worse if I'd *killed* someone.

MGM wouldn't allow Gene to set foot on the lot once we started going together, and for a while Hollywood was swept by rumors that the studio was going to pull me out of the million-dollar extravaganza *Hit the Deck*. But they didn't.

I got an award from *Photoplay* at that trying time. I'm sure the award had been decided on long before, or they would never have given it to me. At the ceremony everybody stayed away from us—way away—we might as well have had leprosy. No one spoke or touched us. That's when I really felt like a pariah.

Lots of Hollywood stars had affairs, got married, divorced, remarried, redivorced . . . all that was nothing new. The difference in my case was my sweet-wholesome-virginal image.

"There were never any pictures of Jane even holding a cocktail glass," one magazine observed. "Unlike some other divorced stars, Jane's life is without preparation for what lies ahead." (They were right, for once.)

For a while I honestly believed divorce *would* wreck my

career—and Gene's, too. At first, we fought our attraction to each other, tried to deny it. "As soon as you make a picture with somebody, right away everybody talks," Gene was quoted as saying.

Geary and I even bought a new, larger house so that the children would have more room. And at the same time, Gene and Miriam finished constructing their new "dream bedroom." Still, the rumors increased.

The weekend the film was completed, Geary and I went to Palm Springs for a vacation. We arrived in cheerful moods on a Sunday afternoon, but by 11:30 that night we had packed and checked out. Two days later I announced in a newspaper story, "Rumors that my husband, Geary Steffen, and I had a misunderstanding are true. We are hoping to work out our problems together." According to *Movie Life*, when that item appeared readers choked on their breakfast cereal.

I planned a personal-appearance tour. The children and Gladys came with me; Geary didn't. Oddly enough, Gene and I frequently found ourselves appearing in the same cities.

Movie Life, ever on the job, reported that during my debut at the Las Vegas Desert Inn, "Geary sat alone at a ringside table" and heard me sing such numbers as "Falling in Love with Love" and "It's Too Late Now." Added the magazine: "If there was a message for him in the titles, Geary heard it straight-faced, applauded and flew home."

Maybe there *was* a message for Geary in the titles.

Some of my dearest friends turned their backs on me. Geary was the poor, deserted husband and I was the irresponsible wife leaving him for someone else, and I guess I was. Also, a lot of my friends were Catholic, and they didn't approve of divorce. Roddy was Catholic, but he stuck by me. (His mother, I'm sure, was appalled by my behavior, but she stuck by me, too. I appreciated that.)

Time does take care of these things. It moves on; the tables do turn. My old friends returned, forgot, and forgave.

The Cocoanut Grove was *the* place to go in Hollywood then. It was like being on a movie set; it even had fake clouds blowing languidly across the ceiling. All the big acts played there, appearing amid the fake palm trees with fake monkeys dangling from them. When we first came to Hollywood, Mama and Daddy and I would go to the Cocoanut Grove for dinner on Sunday nights, and Daddy and I would dance. It was the only place in town a youngster could dance—it was against the law to dance in a club until you were eighteen—but the Grove was different. It seemed like family.

For me, opening there was a moment of triumph at a time when everything was falling apart. It was a chance to change my image, to show the studio that I really *was* a grown-up adult woman.

(But I was scared: *Would* anyone want to come or had my audience turned away along with so many of my friends?)

Well, the Grove appearance was a tremendous success. It took fifteen waiters to carry my flowers, reporters said. Gene was there to support me, of course: I was eagerly waiting for our divorces to become final, eagerly waiting to marry the man I adored. Gene and his mother were seated with Mama and her date, a very young man whose name I never knew. Daddy sat at another table. And the nightclub was filled with Hollywood celebrities: Dore Schary, Debbie Reynolds, Spike and Helen Jones, Rory and Lita Calhoun, Merv Griffin, and many others. "Sensationally unbelievable," raved *The Hollywood Reporter*.

I remember I wore a Helen Rose gown in bright fire-engine red, with layers of petticoats in orange, light orange, hot pink, pale pink, white. It had one chiffon shoulder strap, a fitted waist, and a gorgeous full skirt; and my hair was almost platinum (the "in" color that year). When I danced and the petticoats whirled, I looked like a burning flame, a flaming femme fatale.

I sang the usual songs and when I got to "Most Unusual Day" and the line "My heart won't behave in the usual way," according to a press account, I "looked straight at Nelson and several tab-payers found the look so intimate they blushed a deep red." I doubt that.

I'm sure I did look at Gene that way. And I kept looking at him that way for the next couple of months. But a week before

New Year's Day, 1954, when I arrived at Hollywood's gala end-of-the-year celebration, the man with me wasn't Gene. He hadn't been with me for more than a month.

"We didn't have a fight," I told the press. "The decision was as much Gene's as it was mine."

The decision was entirely Gene's. After my career was nearly ruined, and his career was nearly ruined, after all our friends avoided us, and with the studios outraged, with fans writing furious letters to the magazines, and after Geary and Miriam and our three small children had been hurt—after all that, Gene said he wasn't sure.

"After everything we've gone through, you're not sure?" I was dumbfounded.

"I just want to go away for a little while and think about it," he said.

"You do? You want to think about it? Then go!"

He left, and left me numb, embarrassed, and angry. Very angry. Angry with myself to think I had been so foolish.

I had broken my image all right, I had broken up a lot of things I cared about.

** *11* **

TWO DAYS AFTER Gene walked out of my life, Pat Nerney walked in, walked into my fear of being alone.

Years later, Gene and I became good friends, but a few weeks after he went off to think things over, Pat and I started appearing together at Hollywood social events. A year after Gene decided he wasn't sure, Pat and I got married in Ojai, California.

It's hard to believe now, but it really happened that fast. One day I was shocked, crying, wandering around my big, empty house, unable to understand why Gene had left, and the next thing I knew, the telephone rang and Pat asked me for dinner.

Pat was an auto dealer, who'd once been married to the actress Mona Freeman. When he called he said, "You don't know me but I know you. I used to be married to Mona Freeman, so you've probably seen my name in the papers." I had. I had a vague idea of who he was, but we'd never met. "My name is in the paper all the time," he said. "Would you like to go on a date?" It was an odd sort of introduction, but I thought it was funny.

I'd never been on a blind date before and was very leery. What should I say? As it happened, a friend was visiting when Pat called, and he kept telling me, "Why not, Jane, why not?

Get out, forget what's happened. It's okay." I thought, that's right, *why not*?

That night Pat came to pick me up and before he came in the door—practically before he introduced himself—he kissed me. He said, "There, now we've got *that* over with, we won't have to worry about it when we say good night." I thought that was very funny and laughed. I liked him right away, this Irish leprechaun. He had a wonderful sense of humor and I loved that. I'd never known anybody who could make me laugh like Pat did.

The next day, after our blind date, he brought me a blue raincoat as a gift. I don't know why he picked a raincoat, it wasn't rainy, but he loved to shop and didn't care what he was shopping for. That was the beginning of how he won my heart: a laugh, a kiss, and a raincoat.

From the moment Pat kissed me on the doorstep, we were together. Not living together, of course; I hadn't lived with Gene, either. I don't know if I fell in love with him right away, but it was certainly instant infatuation. I was in love with love all my life: "He asked me to dinner, he must want to marry me."

Because I was so inexperienced and knew so little about men, each time I was attracted to someone, or he was attracted to me, I fell in love. And each time, I felt I should get married—and usually did. Attraction, sex, love, marriage . . . they all went together like bagels and lox.

I did love Pat, but I also loved being in love. I loved having someone to share my life with, someone to talk to, someone to send me flowers. And I couldn't bear being alone.

By February or March 1954, when I was busy working on *Seven Brides for Seven Brothers*, the movie magazines were snapping our pictures and speculating about our relationship. But they weren't sure what was happening: "Since the split with Gene Nelson, Jane hasn't lacked for dates," reported *Movie Life*, adding, "Pat Nerney seems to be a favorite." There were no others, really.

Pat was the man I chose. On November 8, 1954, I married Patrick Nerney. *Seven Brides for Seven Brothers* had premiered in July to marvelous reviews, so I was feeling pretty terrific. I'd also finished work on *Deep in My Heart* and *Athena*, both of which opened in December. Pat and I were married in Ojai and honeymooned in Europe, but I don't have scrapbooks full of clippings about this wedding. Elizabeth wasn't my brides-maid, there was no white gown, no flaming candles or scads of fans or friends. But we still talked about "forever"—and, I still believed it.

Nineteen fifty-four was a whirlwind year. I was optimistic about the future, but I didn't know how soon I'd be on my own, without MGM's support. I didn't know that very soon no one would want me. ("I didn't quit movies," I said later, "they quit me.") I didn't know how much I'd miss it all.

I certainly had no idea, when I was working on *Seven Brides for Seven Brothers*, that the charmingly sensible pioneer girl Milly would be my last really wonderful role in a film.

Seven Brides is the story of the seven handsome but uncivilized Pontipee brothers and the seven pioneer women they took as brides. Set in the year 1850 in the newly settled Oregon territory, it gave us an opportunity to dress up in the height of rustic fashion, including those famous dresses made from secondhand quilts. Howard Keel, the oldest brother, and I fell in love instantly—he liked the way I cooked and chopped wood!—but the rest of the matches were much harder to arrange. (I did my best to teach the brothers something about manners, but it wasn't so easy for mountain boys to charm town girls.) Finally, in a plot twist based on Plutarch's legend about the Sabine women, the brothers simply went to town and abducted their unwilling brides.

The dancing in *Seven Brides*, performed by a troupe including Jacques d'Amboise, Marc Platt, Tommy Rall, Russ Tamblyn, and Matt Mattox, was particularly impressive. Bennett Cerf called it "the most original, exciting, and spirited group dancing I ever have seen on the screen." *The New York Times* described the famous barn-raising scene as a "combination of ballet, acrobatics and a knockdown and drag-out fight" that "should leave audiences panting and cheering."

(Miss Powell, the *Times* added, "sings and acts to the pioneer manner born.")

I had never heard of Jacques d'Amboise before this film. I had never heard of most of the dancers playing the brothers, as a matter of fact. They came mainly from New York—and in the case of Hollywood and New York, the twain rarely met. When we met, Jacques didn't talk at all, so because of his name I assumed that he was French and didn't speak English. It wasn't until I moved back to New York and we met again that I learned he didn't speak French at all—he's American through and through and has a distinctive New York accent.

Howard Keel was someone else I didn't know well before the film. Even though we were costars and on-screen husband and wife, we had surprisingly few scenes together. Later, when we starred together in the *Seven Brides* stage production—and then in *South Pacific* and *I Do I Do*—we did become fairly friendly.

Howard and I had professional problems, but together we made a marvelous package—we were good box office. Also, I really *like* Howard, and I understand he couldn't be more complimentary about me. I think Howard always thought that he should have been a bigger star than he was, and felt frustration and disappointment. Those are feelings most of us have shared at one time or another. We're not all that different. But I'm sure those feelings are gone since Howard's success on *Dallas*.

Seven Brides for Seven Brothers is on all the Hollywood classics lists now—it's "one of the best movie musicals ever produced," according to *Current Biography*—but for a while it wasn't even supposed to be made. The studio was pouring all this money into *Brigadoon* and felt it couldn't afford to do two musical extravaganzas at once, so MGM bigwigs were going to drop it. But Jack Cummings, our producer, talked the studio into doing it. He offered to cut the budget, to economize in every way possible. He pleaded. And of course *Seven Brides* was a big hit, a real sleeper, and *Brigadoon* seemed to disappear. We all felt pretty smug about that.

While I was working on *Seven Brides* Pat was working at his car dealership and hating it. He despised what he was doing—he really wanted to be a writer. His mind was really on the arts, not on cars.

After his divorce from Mona Freeman, Pat went to Europe with his friend Paul Clemens, the well-known painter. They kept a fascinating diary (full of humor and charming sex), and would read it to anyone who would listen. And people said, "This is great. You've got to get it published." So they turned it into a book, quite a successful one, called *The Little Black Book*. (It had originally been titled *Sugar and Spice, or How Little Girls Are Made*.) It was fun.

Pat was about to turn forty. We'd been married awhile. I knew he hated what he was doing, and I felt he shouldn't waste any more of his time doing it. I said, "Honey, since you hate the car business so much, why don't you quit and see if you really can be a writer." So he did. But it didn't work out.

He would wander around the house avoiding pen, paper, and typewriter, and driving everyone crazy. And then he'd get depressed and start to drink. Eventually he realized he would have to find another career, so he went into the stock market.

The month after we got married, two more of my movies premiered, *Athena* and *Deep in My Heart*. In the latter I made just a guest appearance. Vic Damone and I sang "Will You Remember?" and then we disappeared, fast. Lots of big MGM names—including Gene Kelly, Ann Miller, Cyd Charisse, and Howard Keel besides Vic and me—did little bits in this picture (and believe me, they were *little* bits).

I was quite fond of *Athena*, even though the critics generally weren't. The movie was way ahead of its time, with health-food faddists, astrologers, numerologists, and positive thinkers. (It would have done better twenty years later!) *Athena* had a beautiful score, by Hugh Martin and Ralph Blane, and a good cast with all the regulars: Debbie Reynolds, Vic Damone, Louis Calhern. We were like a stock company by then.

Athena was supposed to be a satire of a California health cult. I played Athena, the oldest of seven sisters named for goddesses, and Debbie Reynolds played my younger sister, Minerva. Louis Calhern was our feisty grandpa, who kept getting in the way of my romance with Edmund Purdom and Debbie's pursuit of Vic Damone. The film was just another lighthearted Pasternak production, not brilliant social commentary, but I thought it really deserved a better reception than it got.

The director, Richard Thorpe, didn't seem enthusiastic about the picture. After we finished a scene, he would toss the pages of the script over his shoulder and walk away. That really encouraged the cast.

By early 1955 Pat and I had settled comfortably into our Brentwood home. It was a darling little three-bedroom house I'd bought soon after Pat and I started dating. I loved it. I lived there for twelve years.

I did most of the decorating, but Pat got involved, too; he is very artistic. Pat collected paintings—in fact, he introduced me to a whole new world, the world of art. We had some very good Impressionist paintings mixed in with our modern furniture.

Pat was always interested in the finer things in life. His circle of friends was very different from the people I was used to. They were society people. He grew up with David May of the May Company, and they stayed close as adults. Although Pat ran in rarefied circles, he wasn't in their financial league, and he wanted so much to be. I believe Pat always felt inadequate; money was terribly important to him. He was extremely generous, constantly buying gifts for me and everyone else. It seemed as if he were trying to buy his way into the "inner circle"—and the sad thing was, he was already *in* that circle. Everybody liked him for himself, but I don't think he felt they did.

Pat was, and is, an intelligent, funny, and very charming man, but I don't think he thinks he is. That's what led to his drinking, I'm sure—and what eventually broke up our marriage.

I must have earned more than he did. However, money was never an issue between us. I never knew who earned what. I had no sense about money. I had no idea what it took to live. Someone had always taken care of that problem for me.

Whoever it was hadn't taken care of it *well*, but as long as I didn't have to think about financial things, I was satisfied.

Whenever I married, I put my life entirely in my husband's hands. I turned my life over to him; I let him make all the decisions, while I was the dutiful wife. Even though I may have been supporting us both, I refused to admit it. I never let myself believe I was the breadwinner because that wasn't the way things were supposed to be. I had always secretly accepted the stereotype that the man should support his wife. And so if the man *should* support his wife, my man *was* supporting me.

How foolish all this seems now. All this confusion of money and the sexes really makes no sense.

People assumed that money was a factor in my divorces, but it never was, not once. "Why did you get a divorce?" they would ask. "Was it because of money, because of your success? Was it because you earned more than he did? Was he jealous of your career? Were you disappointed that he didn't make it big?" People always asked those questions . . . but those assumptions were always wrong.

Each time I married, I chose men who were less "successful" than I in the eyes of the world. I was a movie star: Geary was trying to get into the insurance business, Pat was unhappy selling cars, my third husband, Jim was unhappy in public relations, and David (my fourth) was floundering. My need was to "make everything right," just as I did for Mama and Daddy. I'm sure Mama and Daddy would have managed just fine on their own, but as a child I felt that responsibility for them, that need to help; I wanted to please; and later, when I married, it was the same. I see now that I chose men who really *needed* my help. I *liked* that role; I was used to it.

Although I earned a lot of money, my financial situation was often precarious; so when I married Pat, I was starting over for the third time.

My years with Pat were very special. He introduced me to art, to culture, to a whole world I hadn't known anything about. I adapted to that world very quickly. I was a good student. I was an actress and used to learning new parts.

On February 1, 1956—soon after I left MGM—our daughter, Lindsay Averille, was born. I named her Lindsay after Lindsay olives, and Averille after a friend.

G.A. was already four and a half, Sissy was just past three, and Pat's daughter, Monie, was with us a lot, so our small house was alive (and noisy) with the patter of tiny feet. I was thrilled to have another baby; I wanted another child that was ours. I thought Pat did, too, but he was not patient with children. That was one of our biggest problems.

After we married, Pat gave me a beautiful pair of diamond earrings, but they were for pierced ears. My ears were not pierced because I was terrified of needles. If someone even *mentioned* a hypodermic needle, my knees would go weak. I wasn't about to have my ears pierced, even for these earrings, but I told Pat I'd have it done when we had a baby. I figured I would be under anesthesia anyway, so it seemed like the ideal time.

When I found out I was pregnant, I took the earrings to the doctor with me. I told him he could handle my case if he would pierce my ears while I was on the delivery table, and he agreed. When the time came, I went to the hospital and handed the doctor the earrings. He had forgotten all about our deal, but he laughed. I remember coming out of the anesthetic and hearing people shouting, or maybe it just seemed as if they were shouting: "A little higher! No, a little lower!" "To the right." "To the left." The doctor rushed out of the delivery room to a nervous Pat and told him, "That is the most barbaric thing I've ever seen in my life." And left.

I was so glad we finally had our baby, but Pat was very strict. We all have a tendency to treat our children the way we were treated as children, and Pat's family believed children should be seen only occasionally and never heard. He was ten when he was sent off to a prep school, which he hated. His parents were very strict, very controlled. I often asked him, "Why do you treat the children that way when you hated it so much?" And he would answer, "I don't know."

It's not that he was actually cruel to them. He wasn't mean. It was just an attitude he had: He wanted the house run a certain way and everything in its place. I had to have the children bathed and fed and out of the way by dinnertime. He didn't want them around. He didn't like the noise, the mess. I finally got him to agree that we'd all have dinner together a few times a week, but it was hard for him. He was really happier when it was just the two of us.

Everything had to be just right. The magazines, the flowers, me—we all had to be arranged just so. I still had help with the children and the cleaning, and someone to drive them to their piano lessons or tennis lessons in case I was called to work, but I was probably the only woman in our circle who did her own cooking. Whenever we had a dinner party I worried frantically about which silver tray or set of dishes to use or whether my menu was "proper." Those things were so *very* important to Pat. We were invited to households staffed by cooks and butlers and maids, and he wanted to live like that. I tried to run our home as if we did.

I regret some things in my life, but I don't regret that I married Pat: I loved him. And I don't regret any of my other marriages. I'm sorry I married so many times—that still seems unreal—but each relationship, no matter how troubled, has enriched me and has taught me a lot.

In looking back, I wish I hadn't been so emotionally dependent on my husbands, and turned over the responsibility for my life so completely to them. I should not have expected all my happiness to come from them.

✱✱ 12 ✱✱

"I DIDN'T QUIT movies. They quit me."

The words surprised me the first time I said them. It was years later, almost twenty years since I'd walked bravely out MGM's door and into a brick wall. "I didn't quit movies." I spoke the words laughing, during an interview with the critic Rex Reed, but as soon as I heard what I said, the pain came back. I remembered a young woman, finding the world unbelievable and indifferent, a young woman, anxious to try new paths, but discovering dead ends everywhere she turned. This was a bird who had left the nest and didn't know how to fly.

I left the studio in November 1955, a twenty-six-year-old married mother, pregnant with my third child.

I wanted to challenge myself, to explore my talent. Did I even *have* talent? I wasn't sure. Perhaps I could play a femme fatale, or a young mother like myself, or an unhappy woman, or just someone who wasn't so damn immature and *nice* all the time! Perhaps I could do a drama, play someone else, anyone other than The Girl Next Door.

I didn't realize that *she* was the only one anybody wanted. They didn't want *me* at all. And *she* was on her way out the back door.

"Please let me grow up," I'd beg L. B. Mayer, and he would pat me on the head and say, "You will, you will." Each time I went to see him, he'd pat me on the head. In a way, I understood his position: I was his employee, and a very well-paid employee at that. I wasn't resentful, just frustrated. My work was stagnating, no longer satisfying. I wasn't growing artistically, intellectually, or emotionally. I wasn't being allowed to grow.

I wasn't angry at Mayer. In fact, I felt very close to him. L. B. Mayer was a second father to me, a mentor; in a way I loved him. Oh, I'd heard all sorts of terrible stories about him, but I thought he was a wonderful man. People make him sound like an ogre—he has been called "a monster"—but he wasn't like that at all to me. I was his little daughter.

Mayer actually left MGM before I did. I was still there when he was let go and Dore Schary was brought in to run the studio. I thought it was unfair. He had poured his life into the studio and suddenly he was fired. He had built it up and now they were taking it away from him. From then on the studio went down the tubes. It didn't go down because of Louis B. Mayer. It went down because of decisions made after he left.

Schary was a young writer and producer who had done *Battleground*, a heavier, more dramatic kind of film. He certainly had never done musicals; he didn't seem to care for musicals, he wanted change. He was the fair-haired boy who was supposed to revitalize the studio, but things were never the same after Mr. Mayer left.

I went to his office to see him on his last day, and he was in tears. That little white-haired man, always so elegant, impeccably dressed, hadn't shaved, wore no jacket or tie. He looked so small sitting at that big desk in a rumpled white shirt with rolled-up sleeves, blowing his nose and wiping his eyes with a white handkerchief. I had never seen him like that. He said hello and got up from his desk. I hugged him. Arm in arm, we walked over to the big window overlooking the "priority parking" lot. He fiddled with the venetian blinds and stared out. "Janie," he said, "I don't know what I've done, I don't know what's happened. I don't know what's going to happen to me now."

I felt so sad, so helpless, watching that once-powerful man cry. I put my arms around him again, hugged him, and cried, too. I thought about our first meeting a decade earlier, about my endless, terrified walk into his enormous office. How small everything looked now. How shrunken, how defeated, how pitiful he looked now. I left in tears.

I was just a child when I came to the studio, and a married woman when I left. But peculiarly, the studio system made you *more* of a child. You never had to take responsibility for yourself. You never had to make decisions. You never had to think original thoughts. The studio didn't even *want* you to take responsibility or make decisions or think. And I can't blame it. It's much harder to run a business if your employees demand control over their lives. However, I don't regret the way it was at all.

True, I was part of a business—but at the time, I felt Mr. Mayer was family. A normal child doesn't have so many people to please; but we had our parents, the studio, our friends, our fans—really the whole world. "Oh, you're so sweet and wonderful. Stay as sweet at you are," everyone would say. "Don't change. Don't go like the other ones went. Don't do what the others did." I did, and nobody wanted me.

By the time I left I was eager to go: Everything had changed for me. Still, I get angry when I hear other actors blame the studios for all their problems. It really bothered me when Judy Garland used to say, "The studio made me do this, the studio made me do that." Nobody *makes* you do anything. You make your own choices. If you need that security blanket, then it's *you* who have chosen to stay. What were they going to do—kill you if you left? It's our own insecurity that we can't handle. And we can't blame anyone else for that.

I'm sure some of the terrible stories about L. B. Mayer were true, but I often felt the people complaining about him were spoiled. The complaints only seemed to come from the big stars—who all seemed to have trouble in their lives. But to blame it all on him was wrong. Life can be like the game of

Telephone—it starts with a little conversation, a small discussion; you tell one person something and when it comes back to you, it's a completely different story. After a while *you* start believing it.

It's true they drove Judy crazy about her weight. Someone was always taking away her plate, and the studio doctor gave her weight-loss pills. But obviously if you're going to take those pills and drink, you're going to have problems. When I would get a sore throat, the studio doctor would come to see me, but I always refused to take any of his pills—manufacturers' samples that he carried around in his little black bag. Whenever anyone was sick at home, he'd visit them to make sure they were *really* sick, that it wasn't just a ruse. I couldn't stand him, and I knew enough not to take his pills.

Stars like Judy Garland or Lana Turner always seemed to be fighting with the studio. In my opinion, Lana was spoiled; she was late to the set, always complaining, and the studio allowed her to act that way. Sometimes I felt they *expected* stars to behave like that. I'm sure Lana and Judy believed they were great stars, and they were—and I wished at times that I had a little of that quality because I barely believed I was there at all. Maybe that was my salvation.

L. B. Mayer was already gone when my last MGM movie, *Hit the Deck*, appeared early in 1955. I was originally supposed to be in *Love Me or Leave Me*, the story of Ruth Etting—a *much* better film—but I was replaced by Doris Day, something I've always regretted. I really wanted that part, but I think it was difficult for the studio to see me as a nightclub performer. I feel especially bad because just before Ruth Etting died, she told an interviewer that she had wanted me to play her. I was very flattered.

Hit the Deck was a frothy navy musical, a remake of *Follow the Fleet*, the 1936 film starring Fred Astaire and Ginger Rogers. (The story had also been filmed in 1930, with Jack Oakie.) The cast included a lot of old friends—Vic Damone as my sailor sweetheart, Ann Miller as a nightclub hoofer, Debbie Reynolds, as a show dancer, Walter Pidgeon as my admiral dad—but unfortunately the movie was quite mediocre. Russ

Tamblyn, who played my brother, did some terrific, high-energy dancing, and Vic and I sang numbers like "I Know That You Know" and "Sometimes I'm Happy," but I don't think any of us were terribly excited by this one, not even director Roy Rowland.

I was probably thinking more about my romance with Pat than about filming *Hit the Deck*. Debbie had just gotten engaged to Eddie Fisher, so I'm sure she had her mind on other things, too. I remember the day she first came on the set, wearing a beautiful diamond ring and smiling from ear to ear. At the time, Eddie was back east hosting his *Coke Time with Eddie Fisher* TV show, and he was about to go off the air for the summer and visit Debbie in California. She kept telling me that he'd be there in three weeks and I kept wondering why he didn't just fly out the next day. "Three weeks?" I kept saying. "That's a long time. Why so long?" "Well, he's driving out. He's never seen the Grand Canyon," said Debbie. "The Grand Canyon? That shouldn't take three weeks." I thought that was very strange at the time. I was such a romantic—I still am—I couldn't imagine lovers staying apart a day longer than necessary.

We finished work on the picture toward the end of 1954, just before Pat and I got married in Ojai. I didn't make any films in 1955.

The family came first with me. When I went on the road, all the children, including Pat's daughter, Monie, came along. Even when we went on vacation, all the children went with us. They were getting older, and I didn't have to check in with the studio anymore, and Pat was giving some financial support, so I was freer. I felt very strongly that any desires I had could only be gratified if they didn't take time away from the family. If my project could be accomplished while the family was doing something else, then I would do it. I started a few things while the children were at school—a mothers' tennis class, an art class. But many times I'd be called away to work, and the classes would be passed by. I felt guilty if I took any time to myself. If I did that I believed I wasn't being a good mother or a good wife.

Those were very domestic years for me, those eight and a half years of marriage to Pat—for the most part, good years.

My career didn't disappear completely. I did three more movies, summer stock, made nightclub appearances and television specials, but I never made an important film again. There were many appearances in Las Vegas at the Desert Inn and at the Stardust Hotel with Paul Whiteman's orchestra.

Vegas was so different in those days, so exciting. You could go horseback riding out into the desert just across from the Flamingo Hotel. After the show we would all get into our cowboy boots and jeans and ride out a couple of miles for a typical cookout, cowboy style, and watch the sun come up. Imagine. The freeway is there now, along with wall-to-wall hotels.

It was in Las Vegas that I met Howard Hughes. I had not been aware of his complete background (oh God, Jane, grow up!), but I had heard that girls were stashed all over town as his guests. One day someone called me to say Mr. Hughes wanted to meet me. Well, I wasn't about to be stashed, but I was advised not to refuse the invitation, so I agreed to meet him in the hotel lounge between shows. What he didn't know was that joining us in the booth would be several of the chorus kids from the show.

Hughes arrived with his white tennis shoes and dark suit, and he wasn't happy with all the company. But he sat down next to me. It was loud in the lounge, and not very easy to have a quiet conversation. But he talked a lot, holding his hand up to his mouth every time he spoke. I thought he was worried about having bad breath, but I was told later that he didn't want anyone to read his lips.

After our big date, he sent me a ring he bought at the hotel's gift stand. The pursuit was over almost before it began, and I was glad.

Pat and I spent almost every weekend on our boat, a forty-two-foot ketch we called the *Clarion*. I practically raised the children on the boat when they were small. On their short legs they would run (despite our admonitions) on the deck with big life jackets, which they never took off. Lindsay got her first taste of the boat when she was seven weeks old, propped up on a berth surrounded by pillows, staring in the direction of her big brother and sister in those bulky, awkward jackets. (I used to wonder if she thought they were natural parts of the human body.)

I loved the boat. I'd never owned one before, never been on one. Ours had no refrigeration—just ice—and no hot water. But that was no problem: Lindsay's bottles still got sterilized and the cooking was as creative as it was at home. Give me a kitchen or a galley and I'm happy as a clam.

We entertained on the boat all the time. We didn't leave the dock too often, especially when Pat was having cocktails. The children loved the sand and water and, in a way, being tied to the slip made it easier for me. I loved it all.

I prided myself on providing anything any guest could ever want, even to the Polident in the medicine cabinet. At first I thought we would take off for an around-the-world cruise at any minute.

Rock Hudson, Claire Trevor (Bren), Tyrone Power—all had similar boats at the same marina and many times we partied together.

One Saturday Pat surprised me by bringing aboard a guest I hadn't met before, a prominent star. "What will you have to drink, Burt?" Pat asked him. "We have absolutely *everything*!"

"Aquavit," said Burt Lancaster, and poor Pat almost came unglued because there wasn't any. I had never heard of Aquavit, and might never have if it hadn't been for Burt. From then on, the bar, which was Pat's domain, was stocked with lots of Aquavit.

Those were happy times, times I wouldn't trade for anything. G.A. still remembers those days as a rich part of his life.

Geary had remarried by this time and eventually had three more children. Mine and theirs and ours all went to the same school, so in a way we were an extended family, whether we wanted to be or not. They were all at our house every Christmas and on holidays. And whenever I went on the road and they didn't want to go, G.A. and Sissy would stay at Geary's house. I was happy about that.

I enjoyed socializing with Pat. When he drank he got a little *too* outgoing and silly, but I put aside my embarrassment and refused to notice it. This marriage was going to last!

For a while, when the children were young, we got together quite often with Ronald and Nancy Reagan. I had known her slightly at the studio as the actress Nancy Davis, but we didn't become friends until later. Pat and I would see the Reagans about once a month. I remember that their daughter, Patti, was always a concern. Nancy would call me and we would talk about the problems we had with our children and how we should handle them, "Mom talk." Patti and Lindsay were about the same age. One time I invited Patti to a Halloween party I gave for Lindsay. Patti was very unhappy! She didn't like anything we were doing, any of the food, any of the games, so I told her, "Go on home." And she did. That was Patti.

Later, before Ronnie was governor of California—and many years before he was elected president—I would perform at Republican rallies with him. Ronnie was on *General Electric Theater* in those days, and I can remember how he would never fly. Whenever he had to travel for G.E., he would take the train. Once he became governor, he must have done something to control his fear because he started to fly, and look where he went!

Nancy was sweet and a very devoted wife. She adores Ronnie; she always did. They were always holding hands and touching each other, just as they do today. He comes first in her life; and she comes first in his. I went down to Washington recently and had a lovely visit with them, but Nancy looked painfully thin, and I told her so. "I'm just so worried about Ronnie," she said. "I worry about him all the time."

Before I left the studio, Kathryn Grayson and I found ourselves together at social events. I always liked Katie.

It was wonderful to see her again in 1986 when many of us got together to perform at the Academy Awards: June Allyson, Marge Champion, Cyd Charisse, Esther Williams, Leslie

Caron, Debbie, Katie, Ann Miller and I were all there. The Awards were such fun. We had never spent much time with each other, not even during our years at MGM, and now we were all older, more mature, and more secure.

We dressed together, two to a room, partitioned off like my old schoolroom at Metro. We talked, giggled, compared wrinkles, and thoroughly enjoyed each other's company.

Debbie kept us in stitches telling us stories. What a memory she has! She remembers everything. Our gowns were like our dream dresses at Metro, and we thought we all looked great. So did everyone else. It was like our sorority meeting.

Marge Champion told Leslie Caron that she, Marge, was the one who had persuaded Arthur Freed (the producer of *An American in Paris*) that a French girl should play opposite Gene Kelly—not her. "Besides, Gower [Gower Champion, her husband at the time] didn't want to break up our dance act. So, Leslie, you can thank me." Leslie seemed surprised. She hadn't known that before.

People always assumed that Katie Grayson and I were in competition because we were both sopranos and classical singers, but this was not true. She played much more sophisticated roles than I did, so she never got a part that I would have had or vice versa. We didn't actually see each other much because we were both working all the time, but when we did manage to get together we always had a good time.

I thought Katie was so pretty with her little turned-up nose and big brown eyes. I could never understand why she was ashamed of her generous-sized breasts. She was convinced that they were too large and would do anything to hide them. I always thought how lucky she was to be so endowed. It's odd that so many women whose success depends at least partly on appearance so often have something that bothers them about their looks.

I'm very fond of Katie. She's a sweet person, and has a terrific sense of humor. However, she socializes very little, and that's a loss. In fact, I was surprised she agreed to do the Academy Awards.

My decision to leave MGM was the first big decision I ever

made, except for getting married—and it wasn't a very smart one, either.

I really did the studio a favor by leaving because, although I didn't know it at the time, the studio was planning to fire me anyway. Now that Dore Schary had taken over, and they weren't going to be making any more musicals, I was on my way out. I probably beat them by six months. It was my most important decision; but in fact, as usual, the decision had already been made for me.

I'm not a rebellious person. I don't like confrontation; I don't like fighting. And I don't usually plan ahead very much, either. But sometimes, if things get so bad—if I get stuck in a situation I just can't stand—I know I *have* to get out. I don't think much about what's going to happen next, or agonize about options, or wonder where I'll end up. All I know is I have to escape. And whatever happens . . . happens.

That's how I felt when I left MGM; but in fact what happened proved terrifying. For the first time in my life I had to make decisions for myself. For the first time in my life I had to take care of myself. All I'd ever known was the studio. I was protected and guided by it. I hadn't realized how much the studio had taken care of—the singing lessons, publicity, dancing lessons, guidance. I hadn't appreciated the luxury of having all those things when they were in my lap. Where do you go now for these things? I wondered.

I didn't plan to stop working in films. When I left MGM I intended to go to another studio, one that would offer me the parts I wanted. I wanted to develop my talent, to broaden my horizons, not limit them. But to my surprise—my shock—the other studios were going through changes, too. *Everyone* was moving away from musicals, cutting back budgets, thinking about "message" pictures.

It was a very hard time for me. That's why I started doing nightclubs. I had thought I was going to set the world on fire . . . but nobody wanted to light *my* fire . . . or anything else.

I did do a couple of B movies—not knowing they were going to be "B". I'd hoped that they might be a foot in the door to bigger things. I didn't do them for the money; I just wanted to work, and to be wanted. Not being wanted is the worst feeling of all. It's worse than being lonely. When no one wants you, you're not sure you even want yourself.

I matured immeasurably during those years of rejection—but at what cost? Even now the memory hurts. Even now a silent phone makes me wonder: Am I wanted or unwanted?

∗∗ *13* ∗∗

MY LAST THREE films, which I made after I left MGM, were not successful. One *New York Times* appraisal—"a silly, crawling little bore"—could have described all three: The *Times* was describing *The Girl Most Likely,* one of the last movies made by RKO. RKO was closing even as we filmed, and Universal, which eventually released the movie, never bothered to publicize it. All three movies were released in 1958. I'd been married to Pat for nearly four years; Lindsay, our baby, had just turned two.

For the next five years—until Pat and I divorced in 1963—I threw myself into marriage, motherhood, and a new sort of career.

I seemed to have audiences wherever I went, but it was different. It wasn't the movies. I'd never felt like a movie star in the first place—I'd never thought I deserved all that attention—but it was hard to have this different kind of attention and no one to support and guide me. I told interviewers I preferred performing for live audiences—that's what I told myself, too—but in truth I loved the movies. I was just marking time, waiting for "the right picture" to come along. I couldn't believe my film career was over.

I was absolutely thrilled when I was asked to do *Enchanted*

Island. For one thing, I didn't have to sing. I was to do something different, and, even more important, I got to die at the end! If anything was going to establish me as a serious actress, I thought, dying ought to do it.

But by the time *Enchanted Island* appeared, I didn't die after all. My fans wouldn't allow it, the producer said, so they rewrote the script. I played a dark-haired, supposedly dark-skinned native princess on a South Sea island. (My blue eyes were explained away by mentioning a Swede who years before had visited the tribe!) Since the blue eyes were one of the script's high points, *Enchanted Island* was, as you can imagine, a really terrible movie. It was based on the wonderful Herman Melville novel *Typee,* but somehow Melville didn't translate well onto the screen. How could it?—it wasn't really Melville.

During the filming my costar, Dana Andrews, had a problem with alcohol and neither he nor the director, Allan Dwan, demonstrated any interest in the project. Allan Dwan seemed so thoroughly bored that I thought he didn't want to be on the set at all. (He later told an interviewer, "I suffered through it with a drunken actor and a nice girl who didn't belong in it—Jane Powell—she looked false as hell.") My only positive memory of that experience is our wonderful vacation in Acapulco. We were filming on location, and the whole family came with me, even Pat. I remember Lindsay, who was about a year and a half, running into the ocean, holding on to Sissy and G.A.'s hands, laughing, building sand castles, while my head itched under a long black wig. It was worth making the movie just to have the children with me and see them having such a good time. Vacation with pay, I called it. I understood their joy and giggles, the tickling of the waves as they floated over their little bodies, and the squishy sand between their toes.

So many of my happiest moments revolve around water. Even as a small child I was drawn to it. Any kind of water, in fishbowls, bathtubs, toilets, anywhere. When I was a baby we would go to Seaside, Oregon, for the day, and Daddy would hold my hand and laugh as the waves lapped around our legs.

Mama never went in; she stood silently on the beach and worried and watched us, squinting a little in the sun. Daddy couldn't swim, but he loved to jump the waves. Oregon water is always so cold that we'd quickly turn blue and start shivering, but we didn't mind. We were so happy, cavorting like dolphins.

Once, Jerome Courtland, the actor, Roddy and someone else were going to teach me to dive. I never had any fear of water until I was a teenager and went to the beach. I was put into flippers and a mask, and I had a belt with weights strapped around my waist. I plunged into the water with my usual fearlessness, but suddenly the waves came in and the tide started to carry me out. I struggled frantically, helplessly, until Jerry jumped in and rescued me. After that I still loved the ocean, but I learned to have a healthy respect for its power. I find such solace in water. Often, while I drift on the small raft in our pool in Connecticut, my feet dangling over the side, I drift away—where? Many times I can't remember, but it's always restful. I guess it's my form of meditation.

My first post-MGM movie, and the only one I enjoyed making, was *The Girl Most Likely*, a musical remake of the 1941 Ginger Rogers film *Tom, Dick and Harry*. I played a bank clerk dreaming of millionaires and trying to choose among three charming suitors, Cliff Robertson, Keith Andes, and Tommy Noonan. (This "messy little picture," said the *Times*, "seems determined to fritter away a dandy array of talent"—including "the glorious voice of Jane Powell, as a pinheaded heroine to end them all." He was right about the pinhead.) I was sorry that the reviews weren't better, and that Universal just let the film vanish into thin air, because I thought it was a cute picture. But by the time *The Girl Most Likely* finally opened in October 1958—more than a year after we finished work on it—RKO was closed and no one really cared what happened to it. Kaye Ballard, who played my best friend in the film, remarked that *The Girl Most Likely* closed the studio!

Gower Champion's choreography was marvelous. I particularly remember a spectacular water number, which has since been copied by other choreographers; in fact, it's the model for the water dance in the Broadway hit *My One and Only*. Cliff Robertson and I had a silly, corny dream sequence, but I didn't actually get to know him until later. He always seemed to be curled up asleep somewhere in a corner of the set.

Gower Champion was a very talented man, one of the finest choreographers I've ever worked with. He was very creative, very powerful, very sexy . . . and, I think, very confused. His work on *The Girl Most Likely* was wonderful, then he did a tremendously successful nightclub act for me—but years later, when he was supposed to direct me in *Irene*, my Broadway debut, something happened.

Gower was the one who talked me into doing *Irene* in the first place. He suggested me for it, wanted me in it, knew it would be good for me. *Irene* was my first—and so far only—Broadway musical, and Gower told me I'd be terrific for the part. He'd directed Debbie Reynolds in it and I looked forward to working with him; I'd always loved working with Gower.

When we started rehearsing in L.A., I asked him to make a few changes, which he agreed upon and made, no problem. The next thing I knew he went back to New York and I was informed that he wasn't going to direct me. This was only ten days before I opened on Broadway. I had just arrived in New York, excited and scared. I had moved bag and baggage, even carried my recipes and some special brown eggs on my lap, and suddenly he was refusing to direct me. He said I was too difficult, too temperamental to work with. I was stunned. I'd thought we were friends and he was one of my supporters. I heard later that apparently he'd been having legal problems with the producers. He had also been working on another play and was using me as a scapegoat, as an excuse to get out of doing *Irene*.

I was devastated, shocked, and hurt. Here I was doing the show because of him; and suddenly he wasn't there. Well, I picked myself up, dusted myself off, and got another director, Stuart Bishop. I went on to do *Irene*, and it was a big success—but I never saw Gower again. It's never easy for me to let a friendship die. But with Gower I had no choice. He left—and I never looked back.

It wasn't until after I left MGM that I appeared on television. The studios hated television, feared it desperately, and none of the contract stars in Hollywood were permitted even to be *photographed* in front of a TV set. Movies and television were assumed to be archrivals. Hollywood pretended that TV simply didn't exist.

This seems ridiculous today.

I like television. I find it exciting, and when I got a taste of it, I did a lot of guest appearances. They even gave me my own special, sponsored by the Pepsi-Cola Company. We had a terrific cast, including Gwen Verdon, Art Carney, and Steve Lawrence. The show was live and we had a great time until, just as the finale was about over, the whole set fell down. But we finished it. The show must go on!

The first summer stock I did was *Oklahoma* in Dallas. *Oklahoma* was the first Broadway show I had ever seen, and I loved it. When I was offered the part of the lead, Laurie, I was so anxious to do it. I never thought to read the script. What a mistake. Laurie is always talked about but is hardly ever around. I spent much of my time offstage changing hair ribbons. George Schaefer was the director—a wonderful man—and we were confused as to why it was impossible to enlarge Laurie's part, but finally he found out.

When the show was first done, there were many problems with the actress who originally played the role. For some reason they couldn't fire her, so they just wrote her big scenes out of the script.

One actress who played Laurie in one of the show's many casts, was standing in the wings, after having changed her hair bows, waiting to go on. She quietly said to the stage manager, "Well, I guess it's time to go out and shit peppermint sticks again." I know exactly how she felt.

Lindsay was *always* with me and thrilled to be going on the road with her mama. She was coaxed onstage when she was six wearing her little harlequin glasses, during the finale of *The Most Happy Fella*, and grinned her front-toothless smile at the audience like a pro and loved it. She had worn glasses from ages four to ten, hating every minute. The glasses came off after the director of *The Sound of Music* came over with his little girl, who said to Lins, "You'll never get a part with those glasses on." So off they came and her eyes rarely crossed after that.

Those summers with the children were special summers, but lonely ones, too. I remember having dinner at five in the evening and driving to the theater, wherever it happened to be, passing houses, seeing people sitting on their front porches chatting aimlessly, sprinklers spinning, making that wonderful whirling noise . . . smelling the smell of wet grass, and seeing children running through the sprinklers, riding their bikes through the fountains of water; happy children with nothing to do. What a wonderful life for children, I would think. The wonderful freedom of childhood that I had always wanted for myself.

Even today there are certain sounds I love to hear that go back to my childhood. The *clickety-clickety, da-dum, da-dum* songs cars make as they go over a bridge. The sound of a horn in the distance at night, any horn, a foghorn, a train whistle, a car. Lying in my bed and staring at the ceiling with the moon making shadows through the window, I pretend I'm in a cabin in the mountains somewhere. Sometimes, during those summers on the road, I'd listen to cars rush by outside my hotel room and try to imagine I was sleeping by the seaside, listening to the ocean roar.

After the performance and during the day, I would see people walking and sightseeing and coming out of restaurants, and I'd think, *How wonderful to be them. They can go to dinner anytime they want, they don't have to go to the theater, they don't have to perform, they can just vacation, or go home.* To me, that was a thrilling notion. I enjoyed performing, I liked keeping busy, I liked the people, I liked keeping my mind occupied . . . but I dreamed of the day I could *stop*.

Monday, our day off, was travel day; that is, if we didn't leave that Sunday night after the two shows. I usually drove to the next stop so I wouldn't have to wrestle with the bags and the porters and the planes. Also I would have to worry about my poodle pups, December and Dickens, in baggage. I only had two dogs traveling with me at that time, and usually Lindsay and my hairdresser, Jean Rapollo.

We'd drive through little towns in the middle of the night, singing songs and laughing a lot. If we saw a light in a house, particularly at an upstairs window we'd wonder what was wrong, or why hadn't *he* come home from the beer parlor sooner. The stories we used to make up about those windows were the melodramas of the decade.

I learned many years ago to carry some food with me on the road, just in case. Many times my old standbys, peanut butter and jelly, saved tempers and lives. I still love peanut butter and jelly, don't even need a cracker, just my finger or a knife. Peanut butter, jelly, and lick.

This is going to seem odd because I envied those freedoms, but in fact my biggest problem during the long days on the road was *filling* time, not *finding* it. Even when I did clubs, filling time was hard. Once, in Las Vegas, I made ice cream in the bathtub—with a machine, of course. Performing was fine, even fun, but the other twenty-two hours of the day were unending. You can see just so many zoos and walk so many malls. Every night after the show we would rush to the nearest Howard Johnson, hoping it was still open, and have an ice cream cone—that was our biggest excitement of the day. Many times we were too late, it would be closed. After that thrill, it was back to the motel for TV, if the stations hadn't gone off the air at 10:30. I usually had some knitting or embroidery I could do, but those hours away from home in cold unwelcoming motel rooms, with their institutional furniture and dingy framed landscapes, seemed very long . . . and very lonely.

Occasionally other performers in the show would join us, but they had their own interests, their own lives, and often they stayed at the same theater all season and rehearsed the next show during the day, while I arrived for one show only—as the star. There's something about having your name on the marquee over the title of the play that makes people keep their distance. In general, I saw the cast and crew socially at the party I usually gave during the run or after the show on closing night.

Sometimes I made a special friend—one whose life I touched again as we grew older: Sandy, especially—Sandy Sanders—a male dancer on a tour of *South Pacific*. And Ginny Reinas, a singer in the show. We would spend time together on the road, and laugh and talk and window-shop. But when the show was over, I returned to Hollywood and they went home to New York.

Being the star of a road show takes a tremendous amount of energy—and a tremendous amount of responsibility, too. I had to be sure to rest enough, eat enough—but not too much—had to vocalize and be careful not to tire myself. Even if we were performing somewhere wonderful like Hawaii, I couldn't take advantage of it. The children had a marvelous time, but Mom had to be careful. For me, it wasn't a vacation. I couldn't swim too much; I couldn't sit in the sun too much; I could never have dinner in a nice restaurant because of my five o'clock curfew; and never a glass of wine. I just grabbed a quick bite in a local coffee shop and hurried to the theater.

Whenever I traveled, I tried to keep some kind of a connection with home and everything that was going on. I called two or three times a day, ordered the groceries by phone, kept tabs on the children when they weren't with me.

Once, in the 1960s, when I was singing at the Copacabana in New York, Merv Griffin, an old friend, came to see me. He arrived with Harry Belafonte, and the maître d' ushered them to the back of the room, Merv told me years later. Merv said, "No, no, no! We want to sit in the front so Janie can see us." The maître d' said, "You'll be much more comfortable back here." Merv insisted on moving to the front, but Harry said, "Let it be, Merv." They sat at the back of the room. We all know why.

If you kept your eyes open, you could learn a lot of lessons at the Copa. My dressing room was in the hotel next door, so I would take the elevator down to the kitchen and walk through to the club, and while I was waiting to go on stage, I'd go to the chorus girls' room.

One night while I was in there, a man came in, a big muscular man with a gun—he didn't point it as us, he had just dropped in to clean it. And no one, not one of the girls, seemed to notice, but I was unnerved.

When G.A. and Sissy got older—ten or eleven—they didn't want to travel with me anymore. They preferred their friends, their sports—Sissy her horses and G.A. his surfboard—to cramped hotel rooms in strange cities. They preferred spending time with their own friends to hanging around theaters watching their mother, and I didn't blame them.

Sissy and her horses: Horses were her whole life. She got interested in them when she was ten, and from that moment on it was as if she had blinders on—horses were all she could talk about, all she could think about. Even when she drew pictures, they were of horses. She barely spoke unless it was about a horse. She would have slept in the barn if I'd let her. Sissy was very intelligent, an A student without opening a book. I wanted her to go to college to become a veterinarian but she didn't want to go. "I know everything there is to know about horses, and what else is there?" she asked.

Once, when I was working in Hawaii, all the children were there; I even brought a friend for Sissy so she wouldn't be bored. But she just sat on the beach, playing her ukelele, singing one song over and over, mournfully: "Won't You Come Home, Bill Bailey?" Bill Bailey was her horse!

First, horses were a little girl's hobby; then horses became a woman's trade. Sissy eventually became a trainer and riding teacher, a wonderful riding teacher. Joan Rivers's daughter, Melissa, was one of her students. She had her own stable, called "Summerwind." Sissy found her own path and followed it for a long time.

A housekeeper always looked after Sissy and G.A. while I was gone. I talked to them by phone every night. I knew it wasn't fair to force them to go with me. But Lindsay was different; she *wanted* to go. She loved the cast, the costumes, the makeup, all the girly things. Of all my children, Lindsay is the most like me.

So, by the summer of 1963, Lindsay and I were traveling alone. By the summer of 1963, Pat and I had been married for almost nine years—and by that same summer, Pat and I had been divorced.

I loved Pat, but on May 8, 1963, I divorced him. I'm still fond of Pat. He is a warm, generous, funny man; but in the end, his problems with alcohol did us in.

My children were busy with their own lives. My movie career had been over for a long time. My girlhood was certainly over—I'd turned thirty-four that year. It was all over, I sometimes thought.

But really it was just beginning.

✼✼ 14 ✼✼

I MARRIED JAMES Fitzgerald in Sydney, Australia, on June 27, 1965. We'd been dating for a couple of years, on and off. Jim and I had first met when he produced a show for the 1962 Seattle World's Fair; I was still married to Pat. Jim's show, called *A Lovely Way to Spend an Evening,* starred my old friend Vic Damone and featured Stan Kenton's orchestra. It was a memorable production, and certainly a *very* memorable visit to Seattle!

When I met Jim I thought him a handsome man, even distinguished-looking but he seemed cold and I didn't like him. "Who is this pompous ass!" I muttered to myself. He was arrogant and conceited, but within two weeks we were in love. No. Infatuated.

No one breaks up a marriage. I've said that before. But Jim became the excuse, the catalyst, for the breakup with Pat. I never spent any time alone between relationships, always played it safe, always had a bird in the hand. I never found out if I could exist without having a man to lean on, even if in reality he was really leaning on me.

Pat and I separated only a few months after I met Jim. My guilt was too much for me, as it had been with Geary, to continue living with him. For the next couple of years Jim and

I conducted a whirlwind romance. We didn't live together until we were married, but Jim became my manager almost immediately. My summer-stock career really took off as soon as Jim took over—stock was his forte—and pretty soon I was on the road most of the year. In fact, the earliest clipping from my years with him is dated August 21, 1963 (only three months after Pat and I got divorced). JANE POWELL ESTABLISHES HIGHEST GROSS IN SUMMER THEATRE HISTORY trumpets a notice in *Variety* advertising my performance in *The Unsinkable Molly Brown* at the Melodyland Theater in Anaheim, California. At the bottom of the ad in small print is the name of my public relations agency, Fitzgerald and Mamakos.

Our impromptu wedding in the Wayside Chapel at Kings Cross in Sydney, Australia, was attended not only by all three of my children, but by Pat's teenage daughter Monie, as well as all of Sydney. I had taken all four children to Australia for a nightclub engagement I was doing, and then a trip around the world. The *marriage* was an afterthought. "We decided to marry in Australia because of the wonderful times we have had here and the friends we have made," I told the Sydney *Daily Mirror*, but the truth was very different. We never really "decided" to marry at all.

Jim had been in and out of my life during the couple of years we dated. I had also been seeing Paul Clemens, a very dear friend of mine and Pat's. Paul and I had been good friends for years—*just* good friends—but all of a sudden we were more than friends and we didn't want to tell Pat. Paul was his best friend—and not too long before I'd been Pat's wife. It would have been such a blow to him, I felt.

In June and July 1963, I was planning to travel to Australia, where I had some nightclub engagements. First, I was stopping in Hawaii—with the children—to rehearse my new act. And after Australia, the children and I would travel and end up in Greece, where Paul and I were planning to get married! Only Paul and I knew about this; ours was a very private affair.

And a private sorrow: As I walked slowly toward the plane on my way to Hawaii, I turned around to wave a final good-bye to Paul. Suddenly in my mind I saw my father. A new image of my husband-to-be. "What am I doing?" I asked myself, then tried to forget the question.

When I got to my seat, I discovered one red rose—from Jim. I hadn't been *thinking* much about Jim lately—after all, I was in love with Paul—but now, all of a sudden, here he was. Wherever I went, it seemed, somehow he always showed up.

After we'd been in Hawaii for a couple of days, I called Jim on the pretext of thanking him. "I thought you would be here," I said.

"I don't come anymore unless I'm invited," he said.

"Well, you are invited. Why don't you come over and have dinner?" And he did.

He stayed in Hawaii while I rehearsed, and then I went on to Australia with the children. It was a fun, romantic time for us. Jim was back in my life. I'd been worrying about what to tell Paul, but I didn't have much chance to figure it out because almost as soon as I got to Sydney, Paul called. I felt I had to tell him that we wouldn't be getting married after all. It was a dreadful conversation—I was in the middle of an interview when he phoned—not only was a reporter there, but so were all the children. The phone connection was very bad, but for some reason I felt I had to tell him then and there that it was over.

I still feel bad about this. Paul is a wonderful man, a talented painter, a man I still admire. I felt I couldn't marry him, but I wish for both of us that I had been more dignified about it.

After saying good-bye to Paul, I called Jim. "If you want to get married," I said, "I guess you'd better come down here and we'll do it now." He arrived a few days later. I never did make it around the world, and we spent our honeymoon with the four children.

For the next twelve years, until we divorced in 1975, Jim managed my career (in fact, our business relationship lasted longer than our marriage).

Soon I was on the road again, more than ever, and alone.

One time in Hot Springs, Arkansas, when I was doing my nightclub act, the town was sold out; it was racing season and accommodations were scarce. It was around Valentine's Day, my favorite day of the year. My room was painted my "favorite" color—ugh, pea green. There was the usual blue and brown print couch and a tacky kitchen table set in the corner. The windows were high off the ground, impossible to see out of. The trees were bare, and everything was depressing.

Since I couldn't find a flower anywhere in town, I picked weeds from the vacant lots and put them in drinking glasses, Coke bottles, cans, anything I could find, and set them around the room. Something to add a little life.

The newspaper clippings from my travels—from L.A. to Dallas to Waikiki Beach, Hawaii, and from New York to Phoenix to Sydney—fill several fat scrapbooks. Jim must have saved *everything*!

" 'The Jane Powell Show' has rollicking moments. . . . Her deep suntan contrasts effectively with her blue eyes and elaborately coiffed blond hair."—*The Indianapolis Times,* July 28, 1964. I got a bug down my throat that night. The theater was outdoors.

"Jane Powell's 'My Fair Lady' established a double record gross for both a West Coast production of the Lerner-Loewe classic and as the top attraction for the Valley Music Theatre."—*The Hollywood Reporter,* September 15, 1964. That's always been my favorite show.

"Jane Powell flies high as Peter Pan in Sir James Barrie's classic. . . ."—L.A. *Citizen-News,* December 23, 1965. I loved the flying, and I always cried (of course!) when we all clapped hands to keep Tinker Bell alive.

" 'The Unsinkable Molly Brown' is again battling the icy currents of the Atlantic and the still icier currents of Denver society. . . . Miss Powell is racy and earthy and tireless. Also, she is piquant and winsome."—*Los Angeles Herald-Examiner,* January 19, 1966. I always had a ball with Molly.

"Jane Powell, starring in 'The Unsinkable Molly Brown,' broke every existing record for the Phoenix Star Theatre both for single-week and for two-week engagements. . . ."—*Variety,* February 24, 1966.

JANE POWELL BATTLES FLU IN MOLLY ROLE—*Santa Cruz Sentinel,* March 2, 1966.

"In Atlanta for the Theatre Under the Stars' production of

'Carousel' Miss Powell brought two of her three children, Suzanne, 13, and Lindsay, 10, with her for the duration of her appearance. . . ."—*The Atlanta Constitution*, August 3, 1966.

"Jane Powell and a seasoned group of assistants gather their resources for another date with 'The Boy Friend.' . . ."—*Los Angeles Times*, May 18, 1967. Swen Swenson split his britches in this one, and left me onstage to ad lib, alone, for hours it seemed.

JANE POWELL SPARKLES IN "MY FAIR LADY"—*The Indianapolis Star*, July 18, 1967.

"Modeling for a forthcoming fashion show will be actress Jane Powell, who opens Tuesday night in 'The Boy Friend' at Melody Top Theater."—*The Milwaukee Journal*, July 28, 1967.

"When actress Jane Powell came to town this week the enchanted Scottish village of 'Brigadoon' came alive. As she stepped off the plane, the strains of bagpipes filled the air and young lasses began to dance the Highland fling."—*Dallas Morning News*, August 17, 1967.

"'The Sound of Music' wafted from the stage of Honolulu Concert Hall. . . . Let it be said early that Jane Powell has been one of My Favorite Things since she appeared in that stand-out film musical of the 1950s, 'Seven Brides for Seven Brothers.'"—*Honolulu Star-Bulletin*, June 26, 1968.

"Tiny Jane Powell literally stood the Oakdale audience on its feet Monday for applause that lasted fully three minutes after the final lights came up on 'The Sound of Music.'"—*Waterbury* (Ct.) *American*, August 20, 1968. Can't be unhappy with this one.

So many cities, all that running, all that singing—I got so tired! Not of performing—I had plenty of energy for that—but of *having* to perform. After a while I felt like one of those windup toys, clicking and clacking and wobbling around the room. When I ran down, I'd get wound up again.

I was grateful to every critic who wrote a flattering line, and grateful to my generous fans. But my home life was in limbo and so was I.

The truth is, making Jim my manager was a mistake, a big mistake. I loved him. But I should never have let him manage my career.

First of all, he didn't know enough about show business. He wasn't able to get me the kinds of engagements I really wanted and needed. He'd been in public relations, so he'd been around show business for a while, but doing publicity isn't managing. He didn't have his foot in enough doors, his finger in enough pies. People kept telling me he didn't have the contacts he needed to round out a career. He didn't know the right people, and he didn't have the *respect* of the right people, and wouldn't admit that he had a lot to learn.

Even if he'd been more effective, our business arrangement was a real Catch-22. The problem was simple: If I didn't work, he didn't make money—and that equation was *very* literal. For a long time I was his only client. And later, when I wasn't, I was still his biggest ticket. Jim had no money when we married. I was our source of income—mine, his. His job was finding me work. My job was working for us all.

I had no choice. If I didn't work, our partnership would die.

When we first started working together, when I still hoped to do more than tour in musicals, Jim produced a show for me, for *us,* called *Just Twenty—Plus Me.* It was like a Technicolor variety show, like a movie, or TV special. It could have been successful—but unfortunately Jim was unaware of the pitfalls. Our concert tour was not a disaster, but close. The show involved inventive, complicated lighting effects, a dancing, singing chorus, and a ten-piece orchestra playing offstage. I wore a wireless body mike—which was a new invention back in 1963 and far from perfect. It would crackle and whistle or suddenly go dead, so our sound wasn't exactly top quality. Sometimes we'd even get police calls or sirens over the mike! When Anna Maria Alberghetti was in *Carnival,* someone forgot to turn off her wireless mike when she was in the bathroom, and you can imagine the embarrassment. Those mikes are dangerous.

I honestly thought the show was good—but our reviews were not. We were doing one-night stands, and each time critics would review the sound rather than the show. They'd talk about the crackling mike, our dead sound, or, "How dare they use canned music! How insulting not to even have an orchestra!" We *had* an orchestra, but it wasn't onstage. We didn't use one snip of tape, only live music. The reviewers didn't understand what we were trying to do; they couldn't accept something different. So they never really saw the show; they only reviewed the sound and got angry.

The highlight of our tour was supposed to be a one-night, pre-Broadway performance at Carnegie Hall. Newspaper accounts reported that we wouldn't be appearing at Carnegie Hall because of "technical problems." The fact was, the show, as we'd designed it, could not have played Carnegie Hall. It was completely dependent on its lighting effects—and Carnegie Hall doesn't have those kinds of lights and no means to hang any. It's a concert hall. The paper was right. Jim didn't know the difference between a concert hall and a theater. *Just Twenty—Plus Me* ended.

Pretty soon I started having a different sort of "technical" problem—a problem so devastating that it would change my life.

"Does Jane Powell still, after all these years and all those sound tracks, really have stars in her eyes? Or are they just transfixed fading reflections of happier younger days when a star was born? . . . A more recent generation than Miss Powell's , or mine, would say, 'she does her thing,' and she does it well. If often flat."—*San Francisco Examiner,* April 19, 1968.

"The only technical matter worth discussion was that Miss Powell appeared to be having trouble with high notes, going quite flat periodically. She was obviously aware of it, cutting big notes short on occasion, and it is probably a temporary condition."—*San Francisco Chronicle,* April 25, 1968.

I was losing my voice. This gift, my voice, was the one pleasure I knew I could count on—and I was losing it!

What do you do with your life when the one thing that you think sets you apart from the rest—the one thing that makes you special—suddenly fails you? What do you say when people ask, "Do you still sing?" How do you feel? What do you *do* when you can't do the one thing you know how to do?

I was so scared! It wasn't so much that I was losing my voice; I was losing *notes*, losing *control*—and losing my confidence. It was not as though I had gotten lazy, rested on my laurels, stopped practicing; I had *always* taken lessons and *always* tried to keep my voice in shape. But all of a sudden I couldn't do it anymore. I had no range. I had to have my keys lowered, maybe only half a tone, but I noticed it. And other people noticed it. I was flatting, getting hoarse—it was excruciating. Each time I had an engagement, my voice would get progressively worse so that by the end of the week I was constantly singing flat. I couldn't even hear the notes after a while—I thought something was wrong with my ears. It got so I dreaded going onstage. Singing became a torment. To me, to everyone, I felt.

I'm not talking about a temporary problem. As recently as 1983 I gave a concert with Vic Damone, and the reviews were bad. "She looked wonderful while she sang," they all said—and then they went on. . . . Not a pretty picture.

My problem was due to bad teaching. All my life I'd had bad singing teachers, but I didn't know it. Before the concert with Vic I had been studying with someone in New York for almost a year. He had told me I didn't know how to breathe. Well, no one had ever corrected my breathing before, so I figured he must be right. He told me I was doing great. My voice didn't feel right to me as I practiced, but the teacher assured me everything *was* okay and I believed him, as always. I was so psyched up for that 1983 concert. *My teacher says my voice is wonderful,* I thought. *My voice is wonderful!* Even after the concert—he was in the audience—the man told me I'd done magnificently. And I believed him.

It isn't easy finding the right teacher; there are lots of them out there and you usually don't know until it's too late whether they are good or not. One voice coach at MGM told me I had too much vibrato in my voice, and I had to stop it. A vibrato is the "trill" you hear in the notes, a lightness or uniqueness that sets your voice apart from the others. It's ridiculous to tell someone to get rid of their vibrato, but I didn't know that at the time. Because of my "mentor complex," I always assumed the teacher must be right. Many times I would call my teacher long distance to get the reassurance I needed to make it through a performance. But I still never knew if I was doing well or not. The voice was there sometimes, but the confidence was gone.

Before I came to New York to do *Irene* I was studying with one of the most well-known voice teachers in Los Angeles—another mentor. He would have me put my fingers on my larynx to hold it down and try to sing. Crazy!

I was terrified while rehearsing for *Irene*. I was in L.A. practicing the dance numbers, but I couldn't set the keys. I was coming to New York to do a Broadway show and I only had four notes left in my voice! I didn't know what I was going to do. When I arrived I explained my problem to the conductor, Jack Lee, who sent me to a teacher who somehow got me through it. I couldn't sing anything else, but I could do the songs in *Irene*. I'm a good mimic; I could mimic my teacher, but I couldn't do it on my own. It was almost like being a ventriloquist's dummy.

After the concert with Vic I decided I wasn't going to sing again. I hated performing. I couldn't bear being onstage and failing. I was haunted by a constant fear that the notes wouldn't be there. When people said, "I just love your singing," I wanted to die. I wanted to cry. Singing had become so terrifying. I couldn't do it anymore.

After a while I felt guilty; how could I throw away my gift? Losing my voice meant desertion. I'd been deserted before, but losing my voice was like losing my soul.

✲✲ 15 ✲✲

IF THERE WAS anything I valued deeply in my life, it was family, and if there was anything I chose, it was motherhood. I wanted my children, my three babies. I worked for *their* happiness, not my own. How I wanted my children to be happy!

I never knew that someday my son would be a drug addict. I never imagined, when I combed adorable Sissy's Buster Brown haircut, that someday my daughter and I would have any strain. I never thought, when I watched Lindsay run giggling into the ocean, that my baby would ever have problems.

I guess I assumed that if I were a good enough mother, I could *create* their happiness. But I was wrong. I couldn't. No one can.

My problems with G.A. began as soon as I married Jim—maybe the very *day* I married Jim. Before that, everything seemed fine; G.A. was a sweet, friendly, beautiful, and sensitive little boy. Then, all of a sudden, he became an angry, obnoxious, rude thirteen-year-old. He had never been this way before. He was angry—kicking, lashing out, screaming, and storming, unhappy most of the time. We all were.

I realized later that G.A.'s unhappiness was partly my fault.

I made a mistake, but I made it in complete innocence. My mistake was simple and common: During the two years I lived alone with the children, I had made G.A., as the oldest child, the head of the household. From the time he was eleven until he was just about to turn fourteen, my boy became the "man of the house."

He would sit at one end of the dinner table, the father's end, and I would sit at the other. He was the big brother, boss of his two little sisters, and the only male in our small household. In a way, we all deferred to him as the man of the house. It's no wonder he came to believe it. It's no wonder he rebelled when someone else, particularly a man, moved in. He was displaced. Suddenly Jim took everything away from him, including me, he thought.

He never got along with Jim; he never liked him, but I wasn't that aware of it. He never understood—he never wanted to understand—why Geary and I divorced. Somehow he'd accepted my marriage to Pat without any great difficulty, but of course he was only three at the time, not a teenager on the brink of puberty. G.A. always liked Pat. He laughed with him, even called him "Poppy." But he didn't like Jim.

For years, even as a five-year-old, whenever he was angry with me, G.A. would say, "When I'm fourteen and I can choose, I'm going to live with Dad. I'm going to live with my father."

And I would say, "All right, G.A., when you're fourteen you can choose."

And then he'd cry and say, "Oh no, Mommy, I would never leave you, never." But the threat was there.

Finally things got so terrible I felt his bluff had to be called. I didn't want to—Lord knows I didn't—but he was disrupting the whole family constantly. He was unmanageable, unbearable, and mean. He said it was because he didn't like Jim. "He's my husband, G.A.," I would say. "What do you want me to do?" Nothing I said or did helped. I think he thought I would choose him instead of Jim.

It was the hardest thing I ever did, but I honestly felt I had no choice.

I can see the whole scene as though it were yesterday.

We were sitting on a little green-and-white flowered love seat in our lanai, overlooking the pool.

It had been a fiery day, after many fiery days, G.A. was impossible, and I was at my wit's end.

He sat next to me, tense, sullen, angry, and I said, "G.A., were you thinking of living with your father?"

He looked at me, stunned, and stammered out, "Yes, I was."

These words fell out of my mouth: "I think it's a good idea."

He was shocked. So was I.

I didn't want to lose my child. I didn't really want him to go. I called his father; he was surprised and not very pleased at the prospect. But he had always agreed, as I had, that G.A. could make his choice when he was fourteen.

Geary picked him up that night. We were all very tense. Suitcases waited in the hall as Sissy, Lindsay, Jim, Geary, G.A., and I stood with mixed emotions. A lump was in my throat. I felt real fear and uncertainty about the future.

"The door is always open," I told G.A. "Whenever you want to come back and decide to live like a family again. That's all I ask, G.A." He didn't answer, and they left.

The door was open: But from that chilling night in 1965 until just a few years ago, I barely saw my son. When we did talk, we argued; our conversation ended in angry words. He seemed erratic, demanding, strange; he frightened me. His drug problem started about the same time he moved in with Geary, but back then we didn't know anything about drugs. Even if he'd been using drugs around the house, I probably wouldn't have known it. Parents are the last to know.

We tried everything, as did Jim, to help G.A. with his problems. We went to lawyers, family counselors, to the Church. Nothing worked. No one knew what to do. There were no drug rehabilitation programs in those days, and even if there had been, could we have forced G.A. to go? I felt so *desperate*; there was no one to talk to. No one for any parents like us. We all felt the misery.

At one point I went on a talk show, the old *Mike Douglas*

Show. Suddenly, inexplicably, I heard myself discussing G.A.'s problem. I felt that if I couldn't help my son, maybe I could help someone *else*. If hearing about my struggles with G.A. helped another mother cope with her child, then maybe my suffering wasn't completely useless. If listening to The Girl Next Door talk about drugs helped other parents realize they weren't alone, why not? "We're all human beings with problems," I said. "You're not alone with yours," and I told the audience what I had done and where we stood.

Today there are doctors, self-help groups for parents, seminars, and TV talk shows, clinics and halfway houses, but twenty years ago parents had barely heard of drugs. If G.A. was acting oddly, it didn't occur to me to look for signs. I didn't *know* the signs. I'd never even *seen* marijuana or anything like it.

But when G.A. was living with his dad, he was using more than marijuana. I don't know which drugs he used or how many he tried, but I know he almost overdosed four times. I know he once shot up his father's living room with a gun and spent some time in a psychiatric ward. He came to my front door one day in such a rage we had to call the police. And I had a detective living in the house for a while, whenever I went away. I was so worried about the family. I was afraid for the girls' safety. Every morning when Jim went out to start his car, I imagined bombs exploding in his face.

The years blur. Eventually Geary sent G.A. to college, but college was just a place to hang out—a pad. He went to Santa Cruz, Santa Barbara, a few others. I refused to support his drug habit. "I'll give you my time and love," I said, "but I won't support your habit." To Geary, G.A. could do no wrong! "The boy shot up your living room, Geary!" "But he got an A in swimming," Geary would say. G.A. never graduated. He just hung out with his friends, surfed, and . . .

He became a nudist for a while, lived in his car, lived in a tree. (I don't know *how* he lived in a tree, but that's what he said.) At one point he became obsessed with religion. He was a follower, not a leader, and somehow seemed to follow the wrong roads.

He went to jail a couple of times. I visited him there, but wouldn't bail him out. "Tough love," it's called. One time he was jailed for burning the banks in Alta Vista, part of a student political protest. He stumbled in and out of halfway houses, but none of those visits lasted very long. He would sign himself in . . . and then, not much later, sign himself out.

That's all I know: My boy's life was one of chaos and despair. Years of confusion. Fear.

G.A.'s teenage years were the hardest to bear. He was always on my mind. I would think about him. I would try not to talk about him, but I did. Our whole family was off-balance; everything was focused on G.A. Why did G.A. do this? Why did G.A. say that? We almost felt we didn't matter. We couldn't help him—that's all we knew.

If you're a parent, you can imagine my numb despair. All I had ever wanted was a family, a happy family. But here I was, the mother of three, and despite my love we were all short on joy. My son was lost to me. My older daughter had her own private world of boots and britches; she talked to her horses more than to me or anyone.

Through those bad years, on and off, G.A. and I would meet, but we were never at ease. It was constant torment.

I felt guilty, I blamed myself for my children's problems. I think most parents do. We bring them into the world; we feel it's our job to make their lives perfect. But people only learn to be parents by *doing* it, and we make mistakes. Just when you think you've got it, another child comes along and he or she is completely different. Everything you learned from the first child doesn't necessarily work for the rest.

Being a parent is a difficult career and you don't want to fail. These days most people are having children because they really want to, rather than as a response to peer pressure. In my day it was considered peculiar not to have children. "No children? There must be something wrong with you."

Finally, when G.A. was about nineteen, something changed in our relationship. Not that he stopped using drugs; he didn't stop until he was much older. But something changed between us. *I* changed.

He had called me up long distance one morning because he
wanted something. I was in Columbus, Ohio, working. He
called because he wanted a car to drive back to school. I said
no.

"But you have two cars," he said.

"One of them is Jim's, not mine, G.A.," I answered. "I will
give you the money to take a train, but I will not lend you a
car."

He was furious. "I want to see you as soon as you get
home," he said. I could hear his anger bursting through the
phone line. During our conversation I found myself throwing
ashtrays against the wall. That wasn't like me. I'd never shown
anger before, physically. But the ashtrays thudded against the
wall. That's when I decided: Something had to change, and it
did.

I gave it up to God, really, I'm not especially religious, but
in those days I prayed, a lot. I asked God, "What can I do?"
A couple of days later, when G.A. came to see me at home, the
tables turned and a new tack was taken. Usually, when we got
together, I'd stand over him, lecturing him and shaking my
finger—not very wise of me—while he sat, impassive as stone.
The more upset I got, the less emotion he would show. But this
time things were different; this time *I* was the stone and he was
the lecturer and finger-shaker. I sat there calmly and realized
God *had* shown me the way.

I don't know if this made G.A.'s life any better, but it was
the beginning of a new kind of freedom for both of us. It was
the beginning of letting loose, a letting go.

Both girls moved out when they were eighteen to be on their
own. Sissy wanted to start her own stable. She rented a house
with a barn, built stalls, jumps, and fences, gave lessons,
trained and traded horses, anything she could do to be near the
animals she loved. For years she had been distant, solitary,
secretive; in a way, she was gone before she actually left. And
Lindsay, Lindsay always wanted to work. When she was
twelve she took a job wrapping packages at the drugstore. She
always wanted to take care of herself, be on her own.

The girls wanted to be independent—but I'd take care of

some bills, doctor's bills, advance them some money, little things. I bought them cars, a truck for Sissy, but I don't really believe in subsidizing my children. I feel that people who demand to be treated as adults should take responsibility for their lives. A couple of years after she was on her own, Lindsay told me, "If I had known then what I know now, Mom, I never would have left. It isn't easy."

School wasn't easy for Lindsay, either. She always worked terribly hard, but Cs and B minuses were all she could make, and it was frustrating for her. As far as I was concerned, the grades weren't that important, but oh, how she tried.

For a while Lindsay went to Pepperdine College in Malibu, but hadn't realized it was a religious school. "Mom, everyone carries Bibles under their arms," she said. That lasted a year. Lindsay's mind is not academic. It's people she loves. And it's people who love her.

Lindsay has had rough times—growing pains, like all of us. For years she wanted to be an actress, but I don't think she ever understood how difficult it was. Even after watching me work, watching the singers and dancers she'd known on the road, seeing how hard they worked and struggled, somehow none of that really registered. It's a very grueling business; I wouldn't advise anyone to go into it unless they had such a burning desire they couldn't imagine doing anything else. But Lindsay's energies were scattered. Whatever she was involved with always came first—whomever she was involved with always came first. She wasn't dedicated to a career—and even if she had been that doesn't mean she would have made it. Desire just isn't enough.

Many performers often work three or four jobs at once to earn enough money to study. Somehow Lindsay could never manage to get the lessons. "I can't afford them," she'd say. "I can't get off from my job [as a waitress]." But somehow she could go to the beach, buy presents, or help a friend. The desire was there, but not the devotion. Lindsay was usually devoted to a man instead. She hasn't had the best luck in men, but she is loyal and getting smarter all the time. She has experienced and learned a lot. We enjoy each other's company so much, and we think very much alike, Lins and I. Our sense of humor and energy levels are very similar. I don't think we look alike—she is so pretty, looks like a shorter Jane Fonda with long auburn hair—but we *seem* alike. People tell her, "Oh, you look *just* like your mom." She never thought so when she was younger; in fact, she used to ask me if she was adopted.

Lindsay is such a good person, such a giving person, it upsets me to see her unhappy. She's been a waitress much of her life. "I hate it," she said. "If I'm ever going to do anything, I have to give it up"—but it isn't easy to give up. It's hard work, but your time is more or less your own and you can earn good money fairly quickly.

Lindsay's doing odd jobs now. She tries everything. She's a go-getter, anything but lazy. She started her own little catering business a while ago, and this is a girl who couldn't, or wouldn't, make a peanut butter sandwich. But now she's quite a cook, creates her own recipes, and hopes to merchandise a salad dressing she has created. Lins has also taken a course in makeup, thinks she might like to be a theatrical makeup artist, and she is artistic.

Lindsay gives so much to other people, does everything she can to help. I wish I'd had a friend like her when I was young. But she has had her share of disappointments.

"Mom," she said not long ago, "I finally realize you only have yourself."

All my children have had difficulty launching careers.

Sissy was successful with her horses; she was a marvelous trainer, rider, teacher—and was beginning to build a clientele throughout California—but suddenly she gave it all up. Her whole life had been horses, from the time she was ten years old! Why did she give it up? She met a woman, a new friend, and they wanted to try different things before it was too late, Sissy said. They tried being agents, producers, writers, but so far nothing has happened. I have known for a long time that Sissy has had a different life-style, although she didn't tell me directly until a few years ago. I've been asked by friends, "How do you cope with that?" The answer is, it is not a problem for me. Sissy's choices don't affect my life. It's really no one's business but hers.

When she left home at eighteen, I said, "Sissy, if you have a problem and if you ever want to discuss it with me, please do." She didn't say yes and she didn't say no. She didn't say anything, but she understood.

Sissy still doesn't confide in me. I never really know what's going on in her mind. I didn't know she had given up her stable until months after she had sold everything. She disappears, then surfaces from time to time. I wish I knew more about Sis and she wanted to know more about me.

As a baby, she was a sweet, funny, independent child, adored her brother, was constantly holding his hand; she looked so much like me that it was a problem to find her own identity. Later she achieved it through the horses because they were her own discovery.

A straight A student who graduated with honors, but refused to attend her high-school graduation. She said she wasn't interested.

She is an adult now, a beautiful woman in her middle thirties who has seen some rough times.

Our relationship, when we recapture it from time to time, is pleasant, though sometimes strained. But I love her.

Was I a good mother? I tried.

Am I a good mother? I hope so, but at this point, I hope I'm also a good friend.

** 16 **

THE SUN WAS big and orange—turning red as it dropped from the sky. From the terrace of my penthouse suite, the blue lake looked as clear as polished glass. The day had been warm, a glorious Florida day. A few boats sped over the water.

Did I really want to jump? I loved life. How *could* I want to jump? Suddenly, I began to climb over the rail.

I think now that all I wanted was to escape from the loneliness that seemed to follow me, even here in the lush presidential suite at the Contemporary Hotel in Disney World.

I was opening that evening in the hotel's nightclub for a three-week engagement. It was November 1974, only a few weeks after I'd finished doing *Irene,* and I was exhausted. Jim and I had been married for almost a decade; I loved him but something had been going wrong between us. In fact, some of my loneliest moments were the ones we spent together.

My children were gone, or going; my husband seemed to be too busy for me.

I'd spent time in the sun that day, speedboating with Jim, rehearsing, admiring the magnificent view from the terrace. The clouds were beautiful, it was all beautiful, but everything I saw looked dead. I cried all day to myself, not knowing why. Here I was, surrounded by luxury, in a suite almost as big as our house. It seemed I lacked for nothing.

The balcony ran the entire length of our suite. Wrapped in my robe, I suddenly felt odd and dizzy. I saw myself as that fly on the wall—the fly I had always felt like when I was younger.

Jim was inside; I could hear his razor buzzing. It was about five o'clock. I'd already had dinner and was getting ready for a shower, but something kept pulling me to the edge of the balcony.

Jim was planning to leave the next day. He always seemed to be leaving, always going away. I wished that he were staying, or better that I were leaving, too. More than anything, I wanted to go home. After seven months in New York with *Irene,* where I was alone so much, here I was in another strange city, another strange house, another strange *world*.

I had wanted to cancel this engagement—I'd accepted it long before *Irene,* before I'd gotten so tired—but Jim said I couldn't back out, and I knew that if I didn't keep punching the clock, Jim, as my manager, would lose his fifteen percent. What would happen if I quit? I was afraid to find out.

The boats looked so small from my balcony. The ground— far below—was turning a warm golden color. It was peaceful and quiet. A soft breeze made the tears on my cheeks feel cold, and the warm ground pulled me like a magnet. I pictured myself falling, slowly, in strange, stop-time slow motion, to the ground.

Tomorrow Jim would go. What would I do to make the hours pass? Try to sleep late—maybe until ten? Sit in the sun? But too much sun would drain my energy. Wander around, maybe do some needlework; then wait till four or so, and then have my dinner, and get ready for the first show at 8:30. Six days a week.

I found it hard to breathe and moved closer to the rail.

A radio was playing somewhere in the suite. Slowly I put one foot on the bottom rail, and then the other. I felt dizzy, far away, saw myself falling, imagined the ground below accepting me. A dizzy, driving, friendly force was pushing me, but something was making me hold on.

Jim must have called my name; he touched me, then pulled

me back. I fell into his arms, crying, shaking with terror and relief.

He called my doctor in Los Angeles, who thought my condition might be related to menopause. The doctor didn't bother to ask any questions, just prescribed hormone pills. I was taken to a hospital on the grounds of Disney World, where the nurse assumed I had taken drugs. ("Oh, these performers," I heard her mutter.) I missed the opening-night show—my first missed opening ever—but went on the next night and finished my engagement. (The guilt of missing that opening-night performance was almost as terrible for me as that terrifying step to the railing.) Jim left as planned; he said he had business to attend to.

So after all, I was alone again, and no one ever asked me anything, no one ever questioned me. No one ever asked me, *"Why?"* I wonder myself. Sometimes I can still recall that glorious Florida day, the clear blue lake, the reddening sun, and what-could-have-been.

Let me go back a few years. For a long time Jim and I were very happy in our lovely house in Pacific Palisades. Oh, of course, we had problems. But Jim and I were happy together.

Or at least I was happy with him; I loved him.

I didn't know that he was attracted to younger women. I didn't know that eventually he'd start having affairs with younger women. I didn't know he'd end up living with Lindsay's best friend. I certainly didn't know he would make advances to Lindsay!

Jim was not an expressive person. "Still water runs deep," I used to say (but was it deep or merely still?). He was very stoic, very remote, very private. I could never get him to talk about his emotions; I could never get him to talk about *anything* but work, cars, and boats. Once, when we were on our boat, on our way to Catalina, I was reading *Jonathan Livingston Seagull*. I said, "Honey, let me read you this passage. It's so lovely, so touching." I started to read a couple of paragraphs, and Jim said, "I couldn't care less."

He wouldn't listen, couldn't bear to hear about feelings,

even from a *book*. It hurt me that he wouldn't listen and refused to care about something he knew I cared about.

Jim would hug and kiss me, but in ten years of marriage I never saw him nude. I thought that was unusual! I would ask him why and he would say, "I had five sisters," or "I'm just Victorian," or "I can't help it." I thought maybe if you have five sisters that's what happens. How naïve, Jane. One time when I was undressed, he walked in accidentally, apologized, and covered his eyes. "Oh, I'm sorry," he said and walked out!

"That's all right," I said. "I've worked very hard to get this body. You can look." But he always covered his eyes.

You might wonder how such an extremely—even excessively—modest man ended up making advances to my teenage daughter. How could this have gone on without my knowledge? You might wonder . . . I still do. But the truth is, I didn't know.

When Lindsay finally told me, crying all the while, I was stunned, hurt, and numb. She didn't want to tell me. She was worried about *me*. For a long time, she painfully kept her secret. Before she said a word, she made me promise not to divorce Jim. "I have something to tell you, Mama," she said, "but you have to promise you'll never leave Jim." I promised. She knew how lonely I would be without him. That seemed to be her biggest fear.

Lindsay loved Jim, really adored him. They would have wonderful times together. Jim was a very good-looking man, and when the two of them went streaming along together on his motorcycle, or if he picked her up at school, the girls would say, "Oh, your dad is so handsome." Lindsay loved it; it set her apart in a way. His little girl, I thought.

I didn't do anything, as I promised. Jim and I stayed married for several more years. We had good times, some very good times. Lindsay and I never talked about what had happened. I did confront him when she told me, and he confessed, "Yes, it's true. I will never do it again, and I don't want to discuss it anymore." And that was that. We never discussed it again. I was afraid to bring it up.

So I pretended everything was peaceful and perfect. I tried

not to think about that episode, and for a long time I succeeded. I didn't think about it because—and this may sound silly—my daughter told me not to. I do believe it would have been traumatic for her if I had taken steps against him. But who can be sure? Maybe I took the easy way out. Probably both. I was afraid of being alone and also going back on my promise.

Whenever I was away, I would call Jim every day, maybe twice a day, and always after the show. But he wasn't always home. There were lots of excuses, which I believed. "The car broke down," he said. "I stayed at the boat." "I disconnected the phone." It happened often, and each time I believed him.

Besides me, Jim had a few other clients. He represented Jimmie Rodgers for a while, and another act called the Burgundy Street Singers, a group of ten young people. In this group were twin sisters. I didn't suspect a thing; I didn't *want* to suspect a thing. I ignored all the signs.

It wasn't until months later, when Jim and I separated in 1975, that I started putting two and two together. Actually I didn't do much arithmetic on my own. A friend told me about Jim's singing twin. "I couldn't tell you before, Janie," she said, "not while you two were together, but they've been seeing each other for several years." The pieces started to fit. Jim, in my mind, had never cheated on me, thought only of my welfare, was honest and *perfect*. I had conveniently forgotten about his attraction to my daughter. I had felt so guilty about our separation up to that time. It was a monkey off my back to know for a change that there was a cause, temporary or not, and it wasn't just a whim of mine.

As I've said, *Irene* was my big Broadway triumph and my only one so far, but at first I really didn't want to do it. My old friend (and movie sister) Debbie Reynolds was starring in it very successfully when director Gower Champion asked me to take over after Debbie's eleven-month run. Everyone, including my family, wanted me to do it, but I wasn't so sure.

I guess I was afraid of appearing on Broadway. I was worried about my voice. But most of all, I simply didn't want to leave my family. The thought of living alone for seven months in New York was so depressing.

I really fought going, but Jim and the girls insisted. "It will be good for your career," they said. "We will visit often," they said. "I will stay with you as much as possible," Jim said. "It will be a good experience for all of us," they all said. "We will have *fun,*" they said. So I went.

Jim hated New York. Maybe he hated it because I was there, but he seemed to spend most of his time in Philadelphia handling his other acts—his twins—and whenever he *was* with me he was sick. So I lived alone in an elegant town house with two of my little dogs, December and Dickens.

In September 1973 I had bought a new house in California, and somehow that was the beginning of the end. Our home in Pacific Palisades was too big, now that Sissy and G.A. were on their own. So we found a new house in Bel Air, a lovely one with a wonderful view, but Jim didn't like it. That house was never our home.

Our life together seemed one-dimensional. Work. I always seemed to be away somewhere, or he was away somewhere, always working for *us*, whoever *we* were. Jim collected his fifteen percent, and our life together was business. We rarely talked about anything else. We rarely talked at all. We were in a vacuum. But outwardly, to ourselves and others, all was well.

I opened on Broadway in February 1974. Doing *Irene* was stressful: The demands of Broadway, especially if you're the star of the show, are *relentless*. But despite it all, it is worth it. Despite all my misgivings, I'm glad my family sent me, kicking and screaming, off to New York. Broadway was a new experience, one I'm grateful for, and it was a smash hit!

Irene was a frothy family musical. I played Irene O'Dare, a poor Irish girl from Ninth Avenue who learned sophistication from the couturier Madame Lucy, and captured (of course!) a stuffy tycoon. Ron Husmann was my socialite boyfriend, and the marvelous Patsy Kelly played my mother. Patsy was sweet and dear, a powder puff. I loved her so much. I never heard her say a bad word about anyone or anything. She was a saint and gave everything away to anyone in need or not. Patsy had a drinking problem, but never during working hours. She used to collect people. She would say, "Come on now, we're going out, and it's on me this time." It was always on her unless you outsmarted her. She was extremely funny, not particularly in what she said but how and when she said it. The O'Irish wit.

Later, when Patsy was very sick, I used to go to her apartment in Hollywood, to see her and feed her ice cream. I always called her "Mama." I'd hug her and say, "Come on, Mama, eat your ice cream." And she'd stare at me. "Come on, now. I bought you four new kinds." And she'd smile her toothless smile and eat her ice cream. She was in her early seventies when she died. She brightened so many people's lives, particularly mine. I really miss her.

I was very nervous about opening in *Irene*. Before I went on, as I stood waiting for my entrance, I felt Daddy was watching and waiting with me. The reflection from the spotlights gave a golden diffusion to everything around me. It was ethereal. I felt very close to him and I wanted to be so good for him. He would have been proud. He would have been there. And I felt that he was.

Jim, Sissy, Lindsay, and friends from California came for the opening. It was a memorable time; it was *Broadway*.

My vocal problems had made performing so unpredictable that I was never able to relax, even when a particular performance was going well.

I didn't fail—though I *was* a little shaky at first. One critic said I seemed "a trifle uneasy" in one song, "I'm Always Chasing Rainbows"—but sang everything else "charmingly." Another thought I "started out something less than fireworks," but added, "She wooed us and won us, and when it was all over, we rose to our feet cheering."

And the reviewer for WINS Radio was probably completely accurate, though not completely flattering, when he said: "She started slowly, very slowly, but built up to such a climax that she got a standing ovation. She was very nervous at first, a fact exposed by jerky movements and flat singing, but she got better with every scene. . . . The vocal problems were Powell's only real failing but even so she was singing pretty well at the end. . . . By the second act, she was beginning to look like a star."

Part of the reason why I was so terrified at first, was that the opening-night audience was packed with fans and I couldn't bear the thought of disappointing them. When I walked onstage for the first time, the applause lasted so long I didn't know what to do. Even one of the critics said, "The applause that greeted her first entrance went on for an embarrassing length of time." And I *was* embarrassed—delighted but embarrassed. What if I disappointed all those cheering people?

In the end, I was a hit. Most of the reviews were raves—"Broadway history was made," said one critic, praising what she called my "magnificent voice." And my big number, "Alice Blue Gown," brought down the house. I was wearing a luminous blue dress designed especially for me by Donald Brooks. ("She shimmers like the Blue Fairy," said Mel Gussow in *The New York Times*.) Thank God—I didn't fail!

Seven months later, in September, I gave my last performance on Broadway. I started crying (naturally!) in the middle of "Alice Blue Gown" and had to start again from the top. At the end of the show, I got another standing ovation, one that lasted seven minutes, so they say. I was so moved that, guess what?, I started crying all over again.

When the show was over, I was thoroughly exhausted, emotionally drained; all I wanted was some rest. There was no *time* for rest. I finished *Irene* in September, went to Disney World in November, and then in January I would be on the road for the national tour of *Irene*.

"Honey," I said to Jim, "when I get back from this tour I don't want to work anymore. I want to play, take tennis, take yoga, learn something, have a normal life."

Jim patted me on the head and said, "Yes, honey."

I carried a torch for him way past the time it should have burned out, and he remained my manager for more years than I care to think about. But I was afraid to let go. As he told me, "No one wants you," and I believed it.

∗∗ 17 ∗∗

AFTER A DECADE of marriage, much of it happy, I finally left Jim Fitzgerald in 1975. He didn't protest.

Then three years later, on October 21, 1978, I married David Parlour, a producer/writer/adventurer/jack-of-all-trades. The marriage was a mistake, but I was afraid of being alone. We divorced in early 1981, after only a little more than two years of marriage.

David would talk: I think that's what attracted me to him in the first place. I was still married to Jim—still in love with Jim—when I met David, soon after the national tour of *Irene*. He was the associate producer of a videotape I was making and we just started talking—about exercise, nutrition, the body, feelings, everything. *He* liked to talk about feelings!

Jim was off somewhere when the videotape was finished, so I went to the end-of-production party with David. Well, one thing led to another. But if it hadn't been David, it would have been someone else, I'm sure.

I met David in September. At Christmas I told Jim I thought he and I should separate, though I felt a separation wouldn't change things. He agreed; it was what he'd wanted all along. Jim was, and is, endlessly patient. *You* got angry, not him. *You* made the first move, not him. It was never his fault.

David, however, talked about feelings and ideas. He talked to me. He was refreshing, like rain in the desert, and I ran to him without thinking.

He was a very talented man, but never used his talents to their fullest. He was a director, a producer, an artist. He had many talents but was not focused.

He had no money—but that was part of what drew me to him; he wasn't interested in materialistic things. He didn't want *objects*, fancy clothes and cars; he wanted freedom, vacations, play. And I liked that. In many ways he taught me a lot. That David didn't care about money was rare to me, but when he had it, he'd use it to buy even more freedom (and even less work).

David marched to a different drummer, and I admired that. He was a dreamer. His view of life was exhilarating—but ultimately unrealistic for me.

From the beginning, my romance with David was rocky—and maybe a bit bizarre. Something about him frightened me. The children didn't like him, and many of my friends felt the same way. "Be careful, Jane," they said.

David was handsome—very sensuous. He had a little goatee. His deep blue eyes were unusual, knowing, and mysterious. He never lost his temper, but he seemed like a volcano, ready to erupt. He would come into a room quietly and stand in the doorway and watch me. He crept around the house. And sometimes, when I was alone with him, I'd feel a sudden chill.

He was always *watching* everything! He seemed to sleep with his eyes open; occasionally I wondered if he slept at all. Often when he left the house he would come back unexpectedly. Was he trying to catch me at something? I never knew. He collected knives and guns and tiny tape recorders, small enough to be hidden in a pocket. He owned African masks and spears and hung animal skins on the walls. After we separated, I found books on the shelves about weaponry and intelligence operations and disinformation techniques, the sort of literature I always associated with the CIA.

Once he asked me if I'd like to hear a taped conversation

he'd had with his ex-wife. I said no, but then I started wondering, "Is he taping *our* conversations?"

David was interested in people and what made them tick. Although he talked to me, when other people were around he withdrew—present but not involved.

Soon after I started seeing David, he suggested I see his psychiatrist. It was true I needed help. I'd never been to a psychiatrist before. A lot of celebrities went to this doctor, so I assumed he knew what he was doing. (Why I assumed that, I'll never know.)

I told the doctor that my husband, Jim, was perfect, "so there must be something wrong with *me*. My husband never cheats on me, never lies to me. He's honest."

"No one is that perfect," the doctor said.

"*My* husband is."

"We'll see," he muttered.

After a few months the therapist told me that since Jim and I were separated, David should move in with me. "It will be good for you," the doctor said. "It will help your mental growth."

I'd never lived with anybody without being married to him. Besides, what would my children think?

"They aren't children anymore. It will be very good for you psychologically, Jane," the doctor said.

Well, when someone with authority told me to do something, I did it. David moved in that day. I felt later I had been railroaded into it.

Our romance was troubled from the outset. We'd separate, but each time he left I'd get lonely, I'd call him back, and back he'd come. It was so unfair to him. It always came back to loneliness, my nemesis.

I never should have married David, but in many ways our years together were a period of tremendous growth for me, and he had helped me a lot. I was unhappy, yes; but I was determined to change my life. I was determined to *understand* my life, to understand me, to break the patterns.

David's doctor said one thing that made a sharp impression

on me. "What do you really want to do? When you fantasize about your life, what is it that you see?"

"I haven't any idea," I said. "I don't know how to fantasize."

Maybe because I'd spent so many years embodying everyone else's fantasies—maybe because The Girl Next Door was a fantasy—maybe because my own life had been a fantasy—I simply had no idea how to fantasize. What did I want? What did I dream of? I didn't know how to dream. How I had envied those who had a dream, a burning desire to be or do something, like being an actress, a painter, or a doctor, scrimping and saving to work or be a part of that dream. My life didn't work that way. Every time I had a dream it died, so eventually I stopped dreaming.

"Well, go home and fantasize," the doctor said.

I tried but it wasn't easy. Part of the problem was that in the past whenever I anticipated something wonderful, like a vacation, work took it away. Whenever I made exciting plans, I had to cancel them.

Finally I decided I wanted to shoot the rapids in Colorado, see the Grand Canyon on a raft! I'd once seen a picture of someone doing that and it looked exciting; so now this was my fantasy—and I *did* it.

David went with me, and it was the most wonderful vacation I'd ever had. I'll never forget sleeping out under the stars—it was still hot, even at night—drinking, eating campfire food, communing with nature, just feeling free. I almost missed this one, too. At the last minute, the day I was supposed to leave, Jim called with an offer of a singing engagement. But this time I *didn't take it!* I actually said no!

I kept hoping things would get better with David, that things would be more comfortable for us. But things didn't change. I had to *make* changes. I had to hurt David.

Before the end, though, we had some lovely times together. He arranged a wonderful surprise for my fiftieth birthday, April 1, 1979. We'd been on tour with *Seven Brides* and had just come home to California the day before. Birthdays are important to me, but I didn't expect anything special this year; there wasn't time to plan.

But somehow David had managed to invite all my old friends, some of whom I hadn't seen in twenty years. Ann Blyth was there, and Darryl Hickman, Ricardo Montalban, my dear friend Roddy. I was speechless.

Once, David and I were guests at Francis Ford Coppola's fortieth birthday party. Mrs. Coppola had called and invited me. She said I'd always been his favorite movie star when he was growing up, and asked if I would surprise him by being his birthday present.

David and I flew to San Francisco for the party. I had baked Francis some cookies and bread, made homemade jam, and packed up everything in a basket. What do you give a man like that? I remember driving up to their beautiful Victorian house clutching my basket. I can still picture the vast antebellum porch, the swing hanging from a mammoth oak tree in the front yard, the crowd of family and friends sipping wine, children running up and down the steps laughing and screaming. It was a family picture, the "typical" family, the one I had always wanted.

As I got out of the car, Mrs. Coppola greeted me. She is small and friendly. She led me over to Francis, and I said, "I am Jane Powell, your birthday present."

He was so flustered and shy and speechless, I couldn't believe this was the big movie mogul I had heard so much about. He was shorter than I expected, with a dark beard and was wearing his usual wrinkled corduroy pants.

When he was a little boy, he told me, my pictures were pasted all over his room. He was so crushed when I married Geary that he tore them all down!

Here we were, years later, reminiscing like old friends.

Oh yes, David and I had some special times together: our trips to Peru and up the Amazon, to Italy and Greece. But in the end we weren't happy or, let's say, I wasn't. David had never done anything to harm me. He never hurt me in any way. But somehow I was frightened of him.

When I told him I wanted a divorce, he had the look of a

wild animal in his eyes. I had asked a good friend, Ruby, to be in the house with me. She waited in the next room, and I was glad she was there. But I was sorry also. I felt bad about the whole thing, about why I'd married him—using him to keep from being lonely—about divorcing him, about the way I had to do it. I had hurt him deeply.

The tabloids made much of our divorce, especially the fact I paid him alimony, but I was happy to do it. I felt I owed it to him; I had done him an injustice. I had used him, or at least I felt I had used him. I had told myself that I didn't respect him, but what I found out eventually was that I didn't respect myself.

Yes, David taught me a lot. Without him I would never have tried to know myself or have had the nerve to risk adventures and smell the roses. Without him I would never have been ready for the life I have today.

✲✲ *18* ✲✲

FINALLY I ALLOWED myself to be alone after my permanent separation from David. I was actually enjoying finding things out about myself and being on my own. So when Dick Moore—once the child star Dickie Moore—and I met I wasn't looking for or even wanting a romance. I was in a state of freedom and loving it.

Dick had written me asking for an interview for a book he was writing about children in films, *Twinkle, Twinkle, Little Star, but Don't Have Sex or Take the Car*. We had never met, but his letter was impressive, and not only that, he was a good friend of Roddy's. Oddly enough, our paths had never crossed, despite our years in Hollywood and our close mutual friend.

Roddy arranged a dinner for the three of us, to break the ice, so to speak. Dick picked me up at home. Now a public relations executive with his own company in New York, he had just come to town and was very properly dressed. I was not impressed by him. His hair was cropped very short like a German soldier's. I didn't know whether to say heil or hello, but his big brown eyes were as prominent as they had been when he was a famous child star named Dickie. I knew he had appeared in a hundred films or more, and that he had given Shirley Temple her much publicized first screen kiss almost forty years earlier. I tried to imagine that.

We had a wonderful evening. There were no overtones of romance, just three members of a fraternity talking, remembering, laughing, and having a great time. Being the only female, and having had a couple of glasses of wine, made me the talker of the evening, with memories pouring out, happy, almost hysterical at times. But the others didn't seem to mind. Dick was leaving town shortly, so the interview was arranged for the next day. We met for lunch at the Bel Air Hotel, and then went to my house to talk. My defenses were beginning to fade. Dick was so interesting and natural. He was in the midst of getting a divorce, too, so we had things to talk about besides our movie days. The interview went very well, and we made another date for lunch the next day. He took me to a place I had never been: the Grand Central Public Market in downtown L.A. It was fantastic. Loving markets as I do, I was in my glory seeing spices by the barrel, and the butcher shops carrying exotic meats you'd never find at the local butcher in Bel Air. It was fun, and so was he. He left town the following day, but was planning to return and suggested we might have dinner again. Well, we did . . . we did, and he's never left my life.

I guess God was preparing me for the best. But it was different this time. I didn't *need* someone, I just wanted *him*. The phone lines to L.A. and New York were buzzing three or four times a day. Just hearing his voice every day was a thrill. In May he was coming out for a month to work on his book, and we were to spend it at my place at Laguna Beach. I was a bit nervous about it. I had never spent so much time with someone I barely knew, and a houseguest at that. I had never fancied houseguests very much. How was it going to work? How was it going to affect what we already had?

My qualms were unfounded. We had a perfect time in every way, and all my friends loved him, and so did the children. How good that made me feel. We had little parties at the beach, sat in the sun, talked about everything, worked, and thoroughly enjoyed each other's company.

Dick invited me to visit New York and to tour the New England inns. I had never been east except to work and had never toured the inns, which I'd always thought would be fun. And it was. He made everything exciting and adventurous, and still does. This time I was his guest and I liked it. I felt so at home, so comfortable. That summer, our first summer, I arranged to do a nonmusical play, and I had good reasons to do it. First of all, Dick could visit me on weekends because the theater circuit that booked straight plays was in the East. Every Saturday Dick came to visit me. I've never looked forward to Saturday so much, and I didn't have to sing. It was a terrible play, but I loved being east and spending the weekends with Dick more than compensated.

The East was becoming a very important part of me. While I was in *South Pacific* with Howard Keel, I'd made some wonderful friends in the cast and had kept in touch, so when I visited Dick in New York, I would pack up my three pups, Dickens, Suzie, and Bear, and off we would go visiting. My friends Sandy and Ginny would help me at times with dog-walking and sitting so that Dick and I could get away. I don't know what I would have done without Sandy and Ginny, true friends who loved my little family and me.

I loved New York, too, all of it—all the inconveniences, the dirt, the noise, everything. That hasn't changed. Sandy and I became the closest of friends—he was my buddy, my confidant. We would take exercise class together, have lunch or coffee, and talk every day. It was the type of relationship I had never had before and probably will never have again. He was a part of both our lives—Dick's and mine—that was very important to us.

One morning, quite unexpectedly, I asked Dick if he would like me to move east. I had just fixed breakfast for him. He was talking about some arrangements he had made and suggested that possibly he could spend a lot more time on the Coast and still conduct business. Suddenly I heard myself say, "Would it be easier if I moved east?" He looked a bit stunned, as I was, and said, "Well, yes, *would* you?" And without a minute's hesitation, I answered, "Yes, I can live anywhere. It would be very difficult for you to move." And that's how it happened. I have never regretted it for a minute. New York people are so friendly and vital and direct, and there's no isolation, unless you want it. Around every corner lies another country. On our street alone there are Mexican, Italian, and Thai restaurants, a coffee shop, an Oriental greengrocer, a Chinese laundry—you should hear the languages there. It's exciting. I don't even mind the garbage.

The press, which was very complimentary, had a field day with "Dick and Jane." "When will Dick and Jane get married?" One night we were going somewhere, and just as our taxi was pulling away, a dear lady called out to us, "I'm so happy for you both," and threw a kiss. We caught up with her to say thank you, touched that someone would care that much. New York is a rare town. Almost every day some pleasant interruption like that happens. Taxi drivers wave and say, "Hiya, Jane, saw ya last night in one of your old movies, ya look great!" In the elevator mothers say to their children, "You know who this lady is? I used to watch this lady in the movies when I was a little girl." Of course, the children just look at their mommies and wonder what in the world they're talking about!

Life in New York is so different. In California, at home or on the road, I'd hop in a car to do my shopping or business. Now I walk, hail a bus or taxi, and prepare myself in advance for the whole day—usually with a shopping bag. I'd rarely seen a shopping bag until I came to New York to do *Irene*. I associated them with another time and place, but during the run of the show on Broadway, I did some promotion for Macy's. Out of appreciation the store sent me five hundred shopping bags. I didn't know what to do with them, so I took them to the theater. People were grabbing and wrestling to get those bags; you'd have thought I was giving away money. I was fascinated, but soon learned how important shopping bags are to everyday life in New York. I've become the biggest "shlepper" of all, and save them in every size. They have replaced the trunk of my car.

Our first apartment was so small—no, I mean it was tiny. It was a studio apartment. Before I found it, I had asked Dick in what price range I should look. He gave me a figure and I stuck to it. It was very important to him that he paid for our life here, and I respected that. We lived in that studio apartment for three years.

Just as we were moving in, I had to leave to go on tour. I picked out the paint colors, the fabrics, and the couches before I left. Dick had always lived in a neutral setting, but this time it was different! It was orange. "Pumpkin," the paint card said, and the color was everywhere. The shade was darker than I had planned, but I was not about to spend money to change it or even to tell Dick that the pumpkins had gained strength. Our apartment was an eye-opener when you walked in, but it was warm and gay and ours—a haven with a man, a woman, and twelve little pawprints.

Our days were busy—Dick's with his work and mine with running my houses in Bel Air and Laguna by long distance, rearranging my work load, touring a bit, socializing more than I had ever done, taking classes, and loving my new love. I felt free and productive.

Lindsay had a bit of trouble with the distance. I'd always been as near as the phone, if not right at the house. I was still as near as the phone, but she could sense that this move was not just a tour, it was going to be permanent. She liked Dick a lot, but he was taking me away as far as she was concerned. I understood, but I told her, "Honey, usually the children grow up, leave and move away, but this time it was Mama." Dick and I were in L.A. often, and the girls visited us, so I saw them a great deal, but there always was some problem with the house, or the house sitter, or both. Finally, two years ago, I sold everything. I moved the things I wanted back here, got rid of all the rest, and have never regretted it.

The first Christmas I didn't go back to L.A., Sissy came east. Lindsay was not able to come, and G.A. was nowhere to be found. It was a very different Christmas for us all, not like the ones when the children were little, when the house would be decorated with Santa Claus and reindeer, decorations I had collected over the years, red satin bows, a green Christmas tree, and boughs of evergreen strung from pillar to post. In those days there were smells of Christmas everywhere, and there was always a Christmas Eve or Christmas Day party for friends, old and new. Some of my friends had been invited for more than thirty years. That was Christmas to us.

There was always a cookie decorating and coloring contest. I would make Christmas cookies for gifts, about 150 pounds of them in twenty different varieties, including sugar and ginger cookie cutouts so Lindsay could invite her girlfriends over to decorate them. The little girls would take most of them home, and the rest went on our cookie tray. Sissy wasn't interested, she had her horses. The frosting and all the primary colors for the decorations were in the kitchen. Santa, reindeer, snowmen, and Christmas tree were put in separate piles on the breakfast table so everyone could dig in. What a mess the kitchen was, and what a mess those little girls were, with color and frosting everywhere. All the cookies were judged. I was elected to do that. The prettiest, the most authentic, the ugliest, the most colorful, and the gunkiest. Of course, there were prizes for everyone—something silly. For years all the little girls looked forward to that afternoon, and so did I. I can still hear the laughter and the carols playing in the background. The little ones worked so hard and ate so much. Christmas was a happy, sad, glorious, lonesome time.

One year, after I had made my 150 pounds of cookies and the house was ready and decorated like a *Little Women* Christmas, dinner was almost ready, the house was quiet, and I thought, *What is this day about anyway? All this preparation?* "It's a birthday, it's Jesus' birthday," I said out loud. I had time to make a cake. After dinner was finished and people were getting their second wind, it was time for dessert. The lights went low and I carried in the cake, singing "Happy Birthday to You, Happy Birthday to You, Happy Birthday, Dear Jesus, Happy Birthday to You!" Everyone was confused, and wondered where the birthday person was. Finally they understood and said, "Of course, it's a birthday!" This is a tradition I still carry on in our house. It would be wonderful if the children would continue doing it for their families.

Yes, the first Christmas away was very different, with just the three of us—Sissy, Dick, and me. Just before the holiday,

I had my singing engagement near New York with my old friend Vic Damone, so Sissy came back for that. Then we planned to go up north for a white Christmas and stay in some inns in New Hampshire.

I had been studying with a highly recommended singing teacher in New York for a year, and I thought I was doing well. I was working hard on restoring my voice so I would feel comfortable singing in the one-woman show I'd been writing, and also be able to handle whatever else might come my way.

As soon as I finished the concert, we left. The trip was fun, simple, and different. Dick was different, too, quiet and reserved. I chalked it up to the holidays, or perhaps to the intrusion of a third person. It wasn't any of those things. I found out a week later that in the review of my concert with Vic, the critic said my voice was terrible, and Dick hadn't wanted to tell me. He consulted Sandy, and sweet Sandy said, "She's a grown woman, Dick, you've got to show it to her." Finally he did. I was embarrassed, hurt, disappointed, and angry. I'd worked so hard and had trusted the teacher so much. My voice had failed me. I had failed, and I never wanted to sing again.

A friend said, "Before you give it up, Jane, why don't you talk to Marge Rivingston? She's a good teacher."

"They're all supposed to be," I said.

"At least see her."

So I did. I told Marge I didn't want to sing anymore. To have a talent and lose it is depressing, sad, and scary, and I was feeling that way again. Was it worth it even to try? Was singing just for the birds?

I started studying with Marge five years ago, and what was originally a few musical numbers in my "Girl Next Door" lecture program has grown into many more songs and more happy tales. I actually enjoy singing again, and my voice is better than it's been in many years.

One day after my lesson, I thought it would be nice to go to the beach. "The beach?" Dick said. "This isn't California." But he rented a car and we drove to Long Island, after a few—quite a few—wrong turns, only to discover there was no room to park at the beach that he had in mind. I suggested that we return to the city, but by this time he was irritated and determined. "We will stay here someplace, and go to the beach early tomorrow." The next day, we went. It was disastrous, with radios blaring from every direction, no quiet, no privacy, lots of sand blowing in our faces. He was not happy.

Later, back in the city, I admitted it was time to find a house in the country for weekends. Dick was overjoyed. He had always had a place to go to on weekends, but his house on Block Island now belonged to his ex-wife and the small farm he owned was rented and thus not available.

A house in the country—grass, trees, flowers, and the usual collection of bugs and problems that only a house can give you—we missed those things, so we started looking. We wanted a house near the water so that Dick could fish and also one that had room for a garden and a pool, if we were lucky. I didn't know New England, but had always romanticized about it ever since I saw the movie *White Christmas* and heard the song "Weekend in Vermont." North seemed the natural direction to go, so up we went to Connecticut. We looked at many houses, big, old, new, in-between, and finally got a call from our real estate broker, who told us to bring the check-book. There we saw our "Tea Cozy," an old coach house built in 1874. The bedroom, in the original building with a fireplace and a loft surrounded by square old-fashioned windows, was painted barn red. The house has been beautifully enlarged through the years, but it's still small. It is a year-round Christmas house. There is a pool, a garden, a forest, and a push-me pull-you swing in the corner of the yard, watched over by magnificent hemlock, hickory, and maple trees whose leaves are touched by the fading sun, winter and summer. On warm evenings we rock and talk in that childlike swing, a memory I will keep forever.

Rocks—Connecticut's main crop—poke through the soil in the spring like weeds and help to make the beautiful, ever-present stone walls: They also make the gardeners moan. The kitchen was tiny; everything could be reached with just one step. But I loved it and its size didn't prevent my cooking or canning vegetables from Dick's garden. But this year we built an eat-in kitchen, complete with stone fireplace and all the accoutrements that any cook could want. Dick's vegetable garden and my pretty flowerbeds complete the setting.

Dick finally sold his farm, and we kept some of its furniture along with some from my house in Bel Air, and added some other items. So our "Tea Cozy" is furnished eclectically, to say the least: Lots of clocks that chime at different times, furniture and collectibles, all of different nationalities and periods, all seem to fit. I guess I was always preparing myself for our new home together.

Dick is the most understanding person I know, and if he doesn't grasp something at first, he somehow finds a way to clarify it for himself and for me. He tries in every way to grow, to help me grow. He's not afraid to be afraid. He knows it isn't weak to admit weakness, he has no macho hangups. He is the strongest man I know in every way.

I can discuss *anything* with him, and I'm not afraid he'll laugh at me, patronize me, or reject me. I know he's in my corner. Dick doesn't make me feel I'm dumb and simple, and he doesn't pat me on the head in a paternal, pacifying, dismissive way. (He pats me quite a bit lower, as a matter of fact.) He's given me the emotional stability that's always been lacking in my life, he's given me the confidence to explore and express what interests me, and he's given me—roots.

Isn't that a glorious gift to give someone? I don't know if he's aware of all he so willingly gives me, or if he's aware that he even has the ability to do so, but he's such a rare person in so many ways, all the important ways. He has changed my life and has relieved me of so many burdens. Funny, when your burdens are lightened, how much easier it is to help carry someone else's.

Many times when I think I'm right and perfect, Dick shows me my failings and my naïveté, but I don't mind (sometimes). We have *communication:* I don't like the word, but it's the only one I know. We have the trust and understanding that come when the fear is completely gone.

Dick is handsome, attractive, loving, generous, industrious, playful, romantic, all those things; but most of all I respect him and trust him without limit. Our emotions are so in tune. His anxieties are more exaggerated than mine, I think, and in that way I balance him, as he often balances me. He's not perfect; he does the usual things, such as leaving towels unhung, drawers unclosed, and lights turned on, tuning out when he's lost interest—typical man's foibles—but I'm very lucky to find someone who is not afraid to express his feelings. He has given me the most glorious life, the one I wish for everyone. Thank you, darling.

At our house each season is beautiful, and I am always ready for the next one. I can't decide which I prefer. Every season brings different smells from the kitchen, familiar ones—like those of cookies, Thanksgiving and Christmas turkeys, breads and roasts; canning in the summer, fresh vegetables and herbs and fruits from the garden.

I look forward to them all. Winter brings out the bird feeders, and their various tenants—the cardinals, wrens, woodpeckers, all dining in our yard. They even plant our summer sunflowers by being sloppy with the seeds. Most people want to strangle me when I say that I love snow, but I look forward to the white fields and trees and the folks all bundled up with rosy cheeks and runny noses; the children on their sleighs; the quiet; our little dogs' pawprints running up the hill, and those of other animals and birds, leading every which way; and fireplaces crackling inside, with us enjoying the sight.

The fall shows the trees in different colors; the yard, covered with fallen leaves, makes a carpet collage of amber, yellow, red, gold, and brown. Spring is fresh and new. I love to see the bees and the green again.

Our first spring was a hint of happy times to come, and it brought a gift I had prayed for over and over again.

Dick had arranged a surprise birthday party for me, and Sandy was in charge of getting everyone to the house in one piece along with the cake.

It was April first, I had seen my first bee of the season, and Dick took me to a dinner party with our friends. It was lovely and a big surprise. After dinner we came back to the house for cake and suddenly the phone rang. Dick answered it. It was G.A. Dick knew only too well the problems of the past and his look said, "Oh, oh, it's trouble." I took the call in the bedroom. Our friends also knew the situation, so everyone sat on needles and pins, barely making conversation, waiting for the crash.

"Hi, Mom," G.A. said. "I wanted to wish you a happy birthday and let you know I've joined the world." I was speechless. He sounded so good, happy and full of excitement. I recalled other holidays and birthdays, and years when I had never heard from him, and times when I had found it difficult to believe he was my son. "I've joined A.A.," he said. "I'm an alcoholic and I'm taking it one day at a time." I can't remember all of the conversation, but it was long and warm and without the recriminations of the past. I hung up, dazed, walked back numbly into the living room, and announced to my friends "G.A. is getting well." Then I burst into tears. Dick quietly hugged me. We all cried, hugged, and kissed, and realized that one should never say never.

Sandy, of course, knew my feelings very well, and as always unspoken communication bound us together.

G.A. has continued to grow, in his health, his attitude, his spirit. He has found a new life and has given new life to me. He celebrated his first year of sobriety with us in Connecticut three years ago. What a birthday that was!

I love birthdays—anyone's—so adding another year has never been a trauma for me, possibly because I've always looked younger than my years. Dick, who is four years older than I, said that turning twenty-five was the hardest time for him, and Lindsay had her shock at thirty-one.

It was not until I was older, in my forties, that I became aware that I finally *was* older. At times, when I would talk with a new acquaintance and mention my twenty-five-year-old or twenty-eight or twenty-nine-year-old child, the comment was, "Oh, *no*, you couldn't possibly be old enough." Well, that has changed, and it was then I realized "Ah ha, it has arrived, I'm older!" At first it was a bit of a shock, but the shock was fleeting, for every year life does get better. I always wanted to be a grandmother, even before I was a mother. I was told it was more fun.

Now there are a few more creams on the dressing table, and I even get a seat on the bus from a younger person sometimes. I find a few new lumps and bumps, a little crepy skin here and there; and I've had a few little nips and tucks, too, but I still have my smile lines, and the baby crow's feet. I'm not about to give them up, I've worked too hard to get them.

I must have driven everyone crazy when I was younger, rarely sitting down, talking a mile a minute, and always on the move. Not now. I've slowed down a bit.

There are times now when I walk by a window and the light hits my reflection so that I catch a glimpse of an older woman whose face has more flaws than before, whose hair is a bit grayer than before, even with the periodic touch-up, and I observe that the fresh young thing I was has disappeared. But it feels good and I smile, knowing that I finally made it.

One day Sandy called, sounding strange. He didn't want to talk, but he *did* want to talk. He was hesitant and didn't make much sense. Later I called him back, and he sounded a bit better, but wasn't feeling well and was going to see the doctor. I was very concerned. Soon he called to say he had a fever and was going to his sister's for a rest. I had to leave town for several days, to represent a dress line for petite women. My role was to host a fashion show, help ladies with their wardrobe problems, and meet the press in each city. There was a great deal of travel involved. I enjoyed the shows and meeting the ladies who came to see me and to talk about the problems of being a small woman.

It was during one of these tours that Sandy's condition was diagnosed. But we didn't get the word. Dick was out of town at the same time as I. He had arrived home before me to hear a series of disturbing calls from a friend of Sandy's on our answering machine, each one more urgent, more frightening: "Sandy needs to see you." Next day; "Please call me, I have some news about Sandy." "Jane, Dick, I have to talk to you. Please call."

Finally: "Sandy's in bad trouble. We're at the hospital," and then the phone number.

Dick called the hospital as soon as he got back, then he phoned me immediately, and I took the first plane home and rushed to the hospital. The talk with Sandy's friends was evasive, cheerless, uncertain.

Sandy's mother was there. I had met her when I was in New Orleans doing *Chapter Two*. She was a lovely woman, much cherished by her son. She was confused and unbelieving, as was his sister, who had been caring for him.

Sandy was in intensive care, unable to be seen. He had leukemia. It had been so fast, unexpected. We were in shock. Sandy had wasted away, and didn't want to see me, even if he could have, not the way he was, with machines and tubes all over his body. We were all dazed—it was so fast, so fast.

Sandy died two days later. Pneumonia and leukemia is what the doctors told us, and that's what everyone believed. But now we know the truth. When Sandy died, I had barely heard of the dread disease that plagues us all, the disease that has taken so many friends: AIDS.

I don't know if Sandy knew he had it. It doesn't matter. What does matter is that my dear, loving, sweet friend is not with us anymore. I learned later that in one of the last conversations Sandy would have he told a friend not to forget to send me a birthday card, because, no matter what, he would not let my birthday go by without letting me know that I was in his thoughts.

I still feel the pain of not walking and talking with him, of not throwing snowballs in the winter, and picking flowers with him in the spring. As the seasons change and the store windows change, my thoughts of him are ever present. How he loved to window-shop, walk and talk, and plan the next gift we would give each other or a friend. I'd help him pick out clothes that he sent to his mother for no particular reason. And we'd laugh at some of the outlandish styles as we rushed to dance class, our dance bags flying out behind us. There are streets and places and people I can't see even today, the memory is too painful. Ours was a love affair without a romance. We communicated with the "unspoken word," and we still do. Yes, I loved Sandy, and I miss him.

He used to talk about a couple of the soap operas he followed, and said, "Jane, you should do one." Well I did, recently, the soap opera *Loving*. It was quite an experience, and I'm so happy to have done it. I've never been one to watch soap operas, but since being a part of one, my admiration for everyone involved is truly great. It's possibly the hardest work I've ever done, and probably the hardest work in our little world of entertainment there is to do. Constant changes, scant rehearsal, material that leaves an actor wanting more, with few rewards from the powers that be. The fans provide the pats on the back so sorely needed. The cast was helpful and caring, and it stuck together. I stayed on the show for nine months, longer than expected, and all the actors were pros in every way.

My part was fun: Rebeka Beecham, steel-edged, no-nonsense, determined lady—no Miss Goody Two-Shoes kind of character—and I loved her. I thought of myself as a short Barbara Stanwyck, a strong matriarch overseeing the ranch.

On most days, we got to work at eight A.M., having already learned our lines—no TelePrompTers or cue cards on this show—we read scenes with the other actors, got made up, had a run-through with the camera, rehearsed with the camera at eleven, took an hour for lunch, then had dress rehearsal with costumes and props for the first time, notes, costume changes, dialogue changes, then shot until finished. I usually worked four days a week.

There is constant tension on a soap opera. You accomplish in one day what in a normal TV sitcom usually takes a week, and most serious actors feel there is insufficient time to explore and define their character. Each series has several writers, and sometimes your character's basic motivation seems to change from day to day.

I received wonderful letters from fans—fun letters. One lady in Texas wrote often to tell me what everyone was doing behind my back on the days I wasn't on the show. She wanted to warn me. Isn't that sweet?

My dear friend, Ron Parker, the president of my fan club,

also gets many letters. His basement in Oak Park, Illinois, is filled with memorabilia; he has something like six hundred movie magazines and three thousand stills of my films and TV appearances, as well as many old costumes and wigs and props. A reporter once called Ron's house a Jane Powell museum—but to me it's a family scrapbook.

My mother doesn't save old magazines with my picture on the cover and neither do I. But my friend Ron does.

✳✳ *19* ✳✳

IT WAS THE wedding of the year as far as I was concerned, a wedding I thought would never happen, involving a son I thought I might never see or be close to again. And here he was alive, happy, and well. It was a dream come true.

But for weeks before the wedding I wondered why, why, was I feeling so sad, so weepy? Of course, I was happy for G.A. and Maureen. Maureen is a very special person. I had met her on one of my visits to Los Angeles, and she had spent Christmas with us in Connecticut. She seemed perfect for G.A.

With a tinge of irony, I remembered how happy I was the first, second, and third time I married, although not feeling quite the same way about the fourth time. Was I apprehensive because on G.A.'s wedding day I would see his past, *my* past marching before us, or was I fearing the pitfalls that he would have to overcome? Was he strong enough to handle them if necessary? He had gone through so much, had conquered so much. He was at the bottom of the barrel when he decided to climb out and join A.A.

Joining Alcoholics Anonymous saved his life. I really believe that. He missed so much of normal life for so long that now everything seems new. At times, when G.A. first was getting well, he didn't know what to do, what to wear, how to act, how to *feel*. When he started with A.A., he called me one day. "Mom, I want to ask you something. I'm going to go out and look for a job and I don't have any clothes. But you always told me that a blue blazer would take you anyplace, so I thought I would go out and buy myself a blue blazer, a blue shirt, and a navy blue tie. What do you think?"

"You're right," I said, "I think that's a great idea." I was pleased that he had remembered.

Another time, before he was married, he told me he and Maureen had had an argument. I said, "Good."

"Good?" he asked. "Why do you think it's good?"

"You have to have arguments," I told him. "It's normal. If you were happy all the time you'd never know the difference. Life is supposed to have ups and downs."

But there were many times when G.A. wasn't sure. If someone said something that bothered him, he didn't always know how to react. Should he be angry? Should he be intimidated? Should he even comment? There were so many things he wasn't aware of. He'd been disconnected for so long.

Now, as G.A.'s wedding approached, I rejoiced at how far he'd come in four years. So why was I so upset?

"Do you think it's because you're losing your little boy?" Dick asked, somewhat tongue-in-cheek. "Whatever it is, you've been behaving like a pain in the ass."

I broke into tears and laughed at the same time, at the idea of my losing my thirty-six-year-old "little boy," my firstborn. Maybe that was part of it, but I don't think so. What did bother me so much?

Of course, as with every wedding, there were problems, family problems. G.A. and Maureen called one night, so upset by a relative's behavior that they nearly postponed the ceremony. Are things ever different? Everyone gets so wrapped up in himself, old jealousies and injustices come racing from the past to threaten the happy day, the wedding couple's day—a day that should be unmarred by personal differences. More than once I had to stop myself from doing the same thing.

Suddenly I knew what was troubling me: the fear of ghosts. At this wedding, they would all march before me, my whole life practically, the good and bad, even the things and people I preferred not to remember.

There would be Geary, G.A.'s father, his wife and ex-wife (the *other* ex-wife!); Geary's sister, Barbara; my second husband, Pat (Lindsay's father); Fran, my stepmother; and friends from the past who shared the joys and disasters of G.A.'s life. And of course Mama was invited. Would she come?

I think we were all a bit anxious about meeting each other at this mass reunion. Would we behave like civilized adults? What would we *say* to one another?

On the big day the weather was beautiful—a warm October day in Belmont, California, during the Pumpkin Festival. The wedding was held in a charming little Catholic church. The bride directed the rehearsal with a little help from her husband-to-be, and she did it beautifully.

I'm so glad I didn't introduce these two, or this day might not have happened. Usually parents have no taste when it comes to picking spouses for their children. But I'm so glad Maureen is in G.A.'s life.

Dick and I helped as best we could, but it was their day. Maureen was in white, and the bridesmaids were in pastel peach and blue-gray. There were flowers, a rehearsal dinner, a reception—the whole works.

Maureen made the table decorations for the reception; she sprayed the baskets gray-blue to match the colors she had chosen for the bridesmaids, and filled them with pumpkins and strawflowers. It looked glorious, and the bride and groom were beautiful.

The wedding ceremony was free-form and unconventional, but still it was held in a Catholic church. The bride and groom had such a good time; they were unabashed and loving and free. They wanted to "accentuate the positive," as G.A. put it, so he announced to the guests: "If there is anyone who would care to say why these two people *should* be married, please speak up." Dick and I were afraid that no one would say anything, but we were wrong. Many of their friends did respond, and eloquently, as G.A. knew they would.

Such nice friends came from everywhere, some people from G.A.'s past, others from Maureen's. Fran, my stepmother, flew down from Chehalis, Washington. She'd known G.A. as a little tyke when he visited her and Daddy on holidays and vacations in Washington, and also when they visited us. I was so glad she was there. We were all glad she was there. Pat flew up from Los Angeles after receiving a lengthy letter from G.A., reminiscing and telling him how much he, "Poppy," had meant to him. Pat was flattered, surprised, and thrilled, and couldn't miss this day. He was nervous, as usual, so Lindsay— little mother—looked after him as she so often does. Lindsay was the only one of G.A.'s sisters (and a stepsister at that) who came to the wedding. The other sisters and brother—Allyson, Crissy, and Baron—had other things to do, and Sissy was in New York, but no one seemed to miss the absentees.

Geary, Sr., looking quite thin and much older than when I had seen him last, came with his present wife, who seemed nice, and is very well liked by all the family. Geary had told G.A. he didn't want to be in the same room with his two ex-wives. I said that the feeling might be mutual. He was also glad the date had been changed so he wouldn't have to cancel his polo game. Anne, his other ex-wife came. She was just the same, always a part of whatever was going on—"Mother Earth." Barbara, Geary's sister and G.A.'s aunt, had changed very little. Barbara is very attractive, bright, and fun. Ironically, a week before the wedding, I was going through an old cookbook, *The Joy of Cooking*, and there, on the front page, was an inscription with Barbara's name and date, January 31, 1949. A shower gift. Oh, the memories! At the wedding I told her the book was falling apart after so many years, and that I thought of her often. She seemed surprised. Years ago she had been so incensed that I would divorce her brother that she didn't speak to me again until this day. How could I forget her? The past kept flashing by.

Dick and Fran got to know each other better. Fran told him of an incident that happened just before she and Daddy were married: Mama called before their wedding to ask him to take her back, more than twenty years after she had divorced him! He said no.

Poor Mama! Lurching from one moment to the next, she never understood herself. I'm beginning to see things about her more clearly all the time.

Fran was one of the best things that ever happened to Daddy: She taught him how to play, be strong, and be loved.

The ceremony occurred without a hitch, except the bride was late. I think Maureen planned that, too, and it didn't bother her a bit. *Good for her,* I thought. *It's her day!* I felt a touch of envy: As a young woman, I would never have dared to be late, for *anything,* let alone my own wedding.

I suspect there were many stories floating around the room, but G.A.'s and Maureen's thoughts were solidly anchored in the present, happy moment—dancing, singing, and touching each other. I wondered how the others there were feeling, those who marched through our lives: Were they remembering the happy times, or the stressful ones? Were they keeping score? Did any of them think silently, *I was right* or *I was wrong?*

G.A. and Maureen were a little taken aback when, during a pause in the conversation, Mother Jane popped the question "What about grandchildren?" I couldn't believe I said it.

"Not now, Mama, but maybe a couple of years down the road," G.A. said, with a nod to his new wife.

How wonderful to see him so happy, and aware of life now. There is an inner glow in him. Now I think we love each other more than ever.

Mama didn't come to the wedding, but I was beginning to understand her. She wasn't feeling well, she said. She also was getting older, and traveling was difficult.

Ten hours later, the wedding reception at the country club was still going strong. G.A. and Maureen and their friends kept dancing and singing with no sign of slowing down, so the usual protocol of staying until the bride and groom made their getaway didn't seem necessary. The old folks, Dick and I included, began to fade and finally at eleven P.M., we said good night.

We returned to our suite overlooking the ocean, exhausted

but happy after the big event. Splashing waves outside our window reminded me of the days in Laguna when Dick first came to visit me while working on his book. Now, here by the water, another happy adventure together.

I was in Los Angeles recently, doing a guest appearance in *Murder, She Wrote*. I was having a wonderful time, enjoying working with Angela Lansbury and reminiscing about the old days, seeing friends, riding bicycles with Lindsay at the beach, and just plain feeling good.

I called Mama, and to my surprise we had a long conversation. Most of it was about how lonely she was. I suggested that she make a list of the positives and negatives, analyzing how things had been since George died. Our conversation continued. She started to touch on things she had never talked about; she said she was in constant torment. "I *haven't* been a good grandmother, and I really do love you, Janie, I always have," she said. She started to cry. Mama explained why she didn't really want me, didn't want a baby. "It was too soon after we were married, your father was working at a little job, and we lived in a little apartment and there was no money. And I was too young," she said.

I could feel her torment, and I felt so sorry for her. I also understood how she must have felt. I can appreciate Mama now, for the feisty, funny little person that she is. I'm glad I asked her that hard and scary question "Mama, did you want me?" I needed to learn the truth—even if I didn't want to hear it. And she was brave enough to tell me. And I love her for it.

Then was then, and now is now. Mama is entitled to her feelings, her life, and there's really nothing to forgive. Now Mama and I can be friends, understand, and enjoy each other in the remaining time we have. We are both contented now.

I'm home now, in Connecticut, enjoying the change of seasons. The holidays are coming, and I'm hoping for snow. My friends laugh at me. They say if I like the snow so much I'm welcome to come over and shovel their driveways. I tell them, "If you can wait till June, I'll do it."

Yes, every season is my favorite. In spring and summer I

look out of my kitchen window and see my gray-haired "Farmer Brown" mowing, pruning, or planting, followed by our eighteen-year-old dog, Dickens. I marvel at this man who loves the earth, the birds, the trees, red licorice, watermelon, and *me*.

Even though we always said we don't want any more babies or puppies, Dick and I were married in Connecticut on May 21, 1988, at the home of our good friend Jay Spectre.

I've changed a lot since I first began to write these words, and so much has changed for me. I feel like an ostrich who has finally pulled its head out of the sand and loves what it sees. Of course, adding a few years doesn't hurt either. My constant worry, my inadequacies, the guilt and loneliness, even my feeling of being unattractive are almost gone. (When I smile, I don't cover my mouth with my hand anymore—my teeth are crooked, so what?) I love getting older, things get easier every day. Easier, but there is still lots for me to learn.

Onward and upward, Jane. The Girl Next Door has turned into a very happy woman.

CELEBRITIES YOU WANT TO READ ABOUT

___THE DUCHESS OF WINDSOR: THE SECRET LIFE Charles Higham	1-55773-227-2/$5.50
___LIFE WISH Jill Ireland	0-515-09609-1/$4.50
___ELVIS AND ME Priscilla Beaulieu Presley with Sandra Harmon	0-425-09103-1/$4.95
___SUSAN HAYWARD: PORTRAIT OF A SURVIVOR Beverly Linet	0-425-10383-8/$4.95
___PAST IMPERFECT Joan Collins	0-425-07786-1/$3.95
___LIVING WITH THE KENNEDYS: THE JOAN KENNEDY STORY Marcia Chellis	0-515-086991-/$3.95
___MOMMIE DEAREST Christina Crawford	0-425-09844-3/$4.50
___MCQUEEN: THE UNTOLD STORY OF A BAD BOY IN HOLLYWOOD Penina Spiegel	0-425-10486-9/$4.95
___ELIZABETH TAKES OFF Elizabeth Taylor (Trade Size)	0-425-11267-5/$7.95
___LANA: THE INCOMPARABLE MISS LANA TURNER Joe Morella and Edward Z. Epstein	0-425-11322-1/$3.95
___FATHERHOOD Bill Cosby (Trade Size)	0-425-09772-2/$6.95
___DANCING ON MY GRAVE Gelsey Kirkland with Greg Lawrence	0-515-09465-X/$4.50
___MY MOTHER'S KEEPER B.D. Hyman (Bette Davis's daughter)	0-425-08777-8/$4.50
___MOTHER GODDAM Whitney Stine with Bette Davis	0-425-10138-X/$4.95
___PIN-UP: THE TRAGEDY OF BETTY GRABLE Spero Pastos	0-425-10422-2/$3.95
___I'M WITH THE BAND: CONFESSIONS OF A ROCK GROUPIE Pamela Des Barres	0-515-09712-8/$3.95